FILIP OSSELAER

REMCO EVENEPOEL

FULL GAS

Strive for *perfection*

Lannoo

For Patrick and Agna

For Oumi

And for Remco

'He's good, apparently, your son'

(Patrick Lefevere goes out for a meal for the first time with

Remco Evenepoel's father and mother)

FOREWORD

My name is Agna.

I'm Remco's mother.

Lots of people address me like that, it's true: 'You're really the mother of ...?' I see people looking at me and thinking: 'Look, that's his mother!' To be honest, it bothers me sometimes. Of course, I'm proud. Of course, I'm the proud mother of a 24-year-old son. But I was already that from the very first day of my pregnancy. His cycling career hasn't changed that. People sometimes say to me: 'It must be really special, having such a talented son!' But that's not how I view it, not at all. Aren't all parents proud of their child? Surely they are? (Or they should be...). Because all children have their talents, whatever they do, whatever their achievements. All children deserve for their parents to be proud of them, to sing their praises.

No, Remco's life hasn't been without its ups and downs. From a young age he has trodden the most difficult path – that was his own personal choice. During those periods, those phases, it wasn't always easy to fit in with his wishes and slot everything into place. But I dare to say – for all to hear – that together with Patrick, Remco's dad, we did everything we could to make our son happy, to make things go the way they should for the best. Patrick and I often told each other that we never wanted to regret not letting Remco do what he thought he needed to do – Remco would never be able to say that he wasn't allowed to do something. Our family, our close friends know how we feel about this, what our experience of it all has been. And that was all before Remco ever got on a bike. The only thing we expected from him was that he would put in the effort, just as we did, even when we had no idea where he'd end up today. And that effort? That was no problem for Remco, far from it. It was even at the expense of his performance at school. To be honest, that was often to my great annoyance! I could be strict. I believed school was important. I didn't always give in, and then he would go to his dad – perhaps he was a bit of a softer touch, that's in Remco's nature as well. Yes, that's the way it is: as a mother, you tend to look at certain things differently. I'm a dedicated mother.

Remco sets goals for himself. And he's strict, really strict about them. People see the pleasurable moments, the moments of success, after yet another victory, after yet another stunning performance. But there's often a flip side to the medal; there are the disappointments, the crashes, the less successful days. Does the outside world give enough thought to that? Far too little, you know. It was not a matter of course to have to let go of Remco, our child, so early. It wasn't easy to have to miss him so much – and it still isn't. It can be days, weeks even before I can give him a hug, a kiss, and during the busiest periods, even that's not possible – apart from doing it via WhatsApp. On the day of a race, we don't see him, we just can't get near him, and sometimes he doesn't have time for us. Even so, at least we're there for him. Our presence, knowing that we're standing somewhere along the course is enough. Remco senses our support.

Such times apart, they are difficult times. But I know why he's doing it and that helps. It also helps when I see how independent Remco is, still only a youthful 24-year old, a young man who makes the small and the big decisions, making his own way through life's twists and turns. These are the moments when I realise that I wish I could keep that little boy small forever, that I could keep him by my side always – but also the moments when I realise that Remco has spread his wings, and I know that I have to let him go.

I know this about myself: letting go is something I need to work on (and isn't that the case for lots of parents?). I often miss Remco when he's back on the road. I miss Remco when he is once again swallowed up by the persistent demands of others, of the outside world, by the rapid and steep ascent he is experiencing. It's times like that when I want to hold on to him a little more, to watch over his well-being, his happiness – it's not good that others start dictating his life, that others make decisions without taking what he wants into account. I'm aware that sometimes Remco's life is restricted, and he can handle that: Remco is patient, I know that, I feel it. Up to the point when it becomes too much, until he explodes when he's had enough of it. Then, I want just one thing: that he follows his own heart, keeps his eyes wide open, for the rest of his life. That he can continue to enjoy what he does, with the people he loves. I don't think Remco fully understands how much this weighs on my mind, how often I miss having him around for a real conversation about it – that little boy from the past, my son.

At a race, my eyes are looking in all directions at once. As a mother, I see and feel so much. I see the failures, I see the suffering. But I hide my feelings then, or at least as best I can. In that regard, Remco and I are alike: falling and getting back up – don't let it get to you too much, just keep going.

The older I get, the more I realise how quickly the time passes. When I was younger, I didn't dwell on that. And maybe that was a good thing, else we might have made decisions in the family that we (and Remco) would have regretted. That's not the case now. When we were young or younger, we made the right choices. We won't have anything to regret. Remco has now reached the place where he wanted to be. And he's worked hard for that.

He'll continue to do so, right up to the end of his career. As his mother, I just want him to remain happy in everything he does, in everything he undertakes.

Then, with a deep sigh, I'll be able to say: 'My little boy, whom I love with all my heart, has achieved what he worked so hard for.'

Agna

1

PROLOGUE

A warm, sunny day in the north of Italy – the morning of 15 August 2020.

That was the date for the start in Bergamo of the 114th edition of the Tour of Lombardy. The riders will cycle all the way to Como, a distance of 231 kilometres, following a fantastic route that winds up and down through mountains and valleys against a background of stunning scenery featuring lakes, ravines, and babbling streams. The Tour of Lombardy is heavy going and only the best riders win, with only the greats appearing on the honour roll, from Fausto Coppi to Tom Simpson, from Felice Gimondi and Bernard Hinault to Roger De Vlaeminck and Eddy Merckx – it's no place for amateurs.

The Tour of Lombardy is normally the last major classic of the cycling season. That's why the race is poetically called in Italian 'la corsa delle foglie morte', which means 'the race of the falling leaves'. The coronavirus measures were responsible for the beautiful autumn classic being held at the height of summer.

Strange, confused times characterised 2020.

In the middle of March, the world plunged into lockdown. Schools, restaurants, shops, museums, playgrounds, and cafés – all had to close because of coronavirus. Working from home became the norm as you were no longer expected, or indeed allowed, to come to the office. Normal life was put on hold, families lived in bubbles, friends had no choice but to stay away, and loved ones could only see each other remotely on a laptop or iPad screen, or by waving through the window of their home. Stuck in solitary confinement, people died. Was the purpose of seeing each other over the course of a lifetime merely to cause pain? And now a final hug, a last conversation was no longer possible – this was not something we humans were used to. The virus had cast people into a new reality, a frightening reality of remoteness, isolation, ignorance, and uncertainty: what else might happen? Hospitals were bursting at the seams and the healthcare system was pushed to the limit by the 'pandemic', a new word that inveigled its way into everyday vocabulary. Everything that happened is of course familiar to you, dear reader. After all, you lived through it all yourself.

But on 15 August 2020, the world was slowly coming back to life; people were allowed to leave their homes again, still subject to restrictions but it was a start. They could breathe again, and enjoy a modicum of freedom once more – freedom to travel, to eat and drink in company, to enjoy themselves.

There was freedom to race again.

The entire cycling calendar was in a complete mess, with tours and one-day races being rescheduled. On 8 August, Wout van Aert was the winner of Milan-San Remo. In a normal year, this course is the season's first classic. La Primavera. Wout finished ahead of Julian Alaphilippe from France and Michael Matthews from Australia. The Tour of Flanders – yet another Monument – won't take place until 18 October, when it will be won by Dutchman Mathieu van der Poel. Two weeks before that, on 4 October, Slovenian Primož Roglič took victory in Luik-Bastenaken-Luik. Confusing, n'est pas? But wait and see, it gets even more complicated: on 3 October – just a day before the Walloon classic – the Tour of Italy kicked off in Monreale (Sicily), where the 15-kilometre time trial was won by the Italian Filippo Ganna. On 25 October, the Brit Tao Geoghegan Hart took the pink jersey. He won the Giro, 39 seconds ahead of Australian Jay Hindley. But – can't you just sense it coming, there's even more confusion with the Tour of Spain also starting in the meantime on 20 October. Still following? A big tour in the midst of another big tour? Can it get any crazier? The Vuelta was won on 8 November by Primož Roglič. And, moving on, yet another change: having been scheduled for 25 October after all the rescheduling, in the end Paris-Roubaix was simply cancelled. Was riding over the cobbles thought to be too dangerous in the middle of autumn? Or was the virus once again too rampant? The Tour de France had also taken place meanwhile, from

29 August to 20 September, with Slovenian Tadej Pogačar the winner of that Tour.

That's just the kind of year it was.

But back to 15 August: Remco was one of the favourites in Lombardy. That was no surprise since in the races that did take place on schedule in 2020, he had been exceptionally good. He'd won the Tour of San Juan, the Tour of the Algarve, the Tour of Burgos, and the Tour of Poland as well. Born on 25 January 2000, Remco was then 20 years old. In mid-August, he crowned his already glittering season with a victory in Lombardy. The newspapers were at least able to agree on that: Remco was in form, Remco was going to win. Remco himself was also convinced and had expressed this ambition – the self-belief was present. Of course he believed in himself.

Even so, it didn't feel right, something was off.

'No, it didn't feel right,' says Patrick, Remco's father, some 4 years later. 'It was true, it didn't feel right.' Patrick arrived in Bergamo in the morning along with his wife Agna, best friends Pascal and Nadine, and daughter-in-law Oumi. They were met there by people they knew, people from the entourage of the Deceuninck-Quick Step team. Joeri De Knop from *Het Laatste Nieuws*, the Flemish newspaper, welcomed them. Patrick has known Joeri for a long time and has a good relationship with the journalist. There were others there too and it was busy in the vicinity of the hotel, with people getting in each other's way – the race was about to start and the sun was shining. Camera crews were present from VTM, the commercial television channel from the Evenepoel family's home country, but that didn't bother them as a documentary was being made about Remco. Patrick, Agna, and Oumi had got used to their presence and knew by now how to deal with all the attention. It was part and parcel of the fact that Remco had gradually become a celebrity.

'But Agna said that something wasn't right,' says Patrick.

What was it though?

In a departure from their normal habit, Patrick, Agna, and Oumi went to the team bus just before the start. What was going on? 'Remco had sent us a message,' Patrick recounts. 'He wanted to see us for a moment. Just before setting off.' They were warmly welcomed there at the start and there was no fuss from the organisers who told them to go through, no problem. 'We could go wherever we wanted and I bumped into Joxean Matxin Fernández from UAE, whom I knew from the past when he was a scout for Quick Step. He said to me, "Have a good race later," and some other small talk, you know how it is. It was hectic, there around the bus.' He pauses, taking a moment to gather his thoughts: 'Things weren't right. No, *that's putting it too strongly*. It seemed like... Well, what did it seem like? We'd arrived OK, we'd flown there in the morning, the weather was nice, you couldn't fault it. And yet: Agna had a nasty feeling. How come? I don't know. It's something Agna has, a gift, something special. She senses things. I don't know how she does it.'

Patrick scrolls through the photos on his mobile. There they are: the pictures from 15 August 2020, Bergamo, Italy. 'Look,' he points, 'here we are standing next to Remco. And here, that's us hugging him.' Why is a family so intensely intimate before the race begins? Because a person is glad to see their child, their son, their loved one. Because something is going to happen, perhaps. That's probably it: a person senses it, they don't know exactly when and where it will happen, but it's coming, that much is certain.

The race started and the Evenepoel family made their way along the course, wanting to follow how the competition would develop. They saw the riders go past twice and each time Remco gave the thumbs-up. Rushing by, he'd recognized Patrick, Agna, Oumi, and the friends –

everything was going well. There was another 100 kilometres or so to go.

'In the meantime, we'd arrived at Luca Paolini's coffee house,' says Patrick. Paolini was a former professional cyclist, the man with the ragged beard who'd won the 2015 Gent-Wevelgem, the edition with awful weather, persevering through rain and wind, over slippery cobblestones, over Casselberg and Monteberg, *In Flanders Fields*, a war zone in times of storm and adversity, where riders were blown off their bikes – Gert Steegmans ended up in a ditch; you can find the footage on the internet. Paolini was removed from the 2015 Tour after being caught using cocaine. After an eighteen-month suspension and at the age of 40, he found himself without a team. As the media put it at the time, '*Dopo la squalifica, la nuova vita di Luca Paolini riparte da un bar di Como*'. 'Following his suspension, Luca Paolini is starting a new life and opening a bar in Como.' Sitting there were Patrick, Agna, Oumi, and people from the team's staff – general manager Patrick Lefevere, Alesandro Tegner, the team's communications manager. Also accompanied by some UCI members and Gianni Bugno, the former world champion. They watched the tour on television while having a cup of coffee. There was still another 50 kilometres to ride.

And then it happened all of a sudden: the disaster.

The riders had ascended the Muro di Sormano, and a leading group of seven strong men had formed: Vincenzo Nibali, Bauke Mollema and Giulio Ciccone from Trek Segafredo; George Bennett from Jumbo-Visma; Aleksandr Vlasov and Jakob Fuglsang from Astana Pro Team.

And Remco Evenepoel from Deceuninck-Quick Step.

As soon as they were below, having completed the few minutes of descent, it would still be a good 40 kilometres to Como. In around an hour, that was where one of the seven leaders would win the Tour of Lombardy.

'Dries Devenyns, the super domestique, had set up Remco perfectly,' recounts Patrick. 'Remco started the descent in the lead.' But he decided to drop back. Was that a spur-of-the-moment decision? In any case: Nibali, a master of descent, was now in the lead. Remco followed, behind. This was not the place where the race would be won and Remco would be better off conserving his energy now, as he'd need it soon enough since there would have to be a breakaway before long, and perhaps a sprint.

Patrick had just taken another sip of his coffee.

'When I looked at the screen again, I saw Remco's bike up against that wall. Agna wasn't sure at first but I knew it immediately: that's Remco's bike,' he says. 'Remco himself was nowhere to be seen.' Looking back, Patrick thinks it was weird: at first he did nothing, kept calm and stared at the bike, the bike up against the wall.

Then began nine minutes of not knowing. Nine minutes of no news, of staring at the TV, of concern for Oumi, nine minutes of silence, of waiting for a phone call that came eventually. A call from *Brama* – Davide Bramati, the team manager who was accompanying the race. He said they'd found Remco. And reported that he was conscious. What goes through someone's head at a time like that? You just stop thinking then, according to Patrick. 'No, then you can't think of anything else. Or rather: all you can think is: he's all right, he's all right.'

Thank goodness: Remco was all right.
Or maybe not?

Patrick heaves a sigh, and swallows. He thinks back to the hours that followed.

Accompanied by the police, Remco's loved ones set off for the hospital in Bergamo. To be truthful, they didn't know what to expect. Remco was conscious when they put him in the ambulance, that much was known. But was that still the case? 'We simply didn't know,' says Patrick. 'And we weren't allowed inside the hospital. The issues with coronavirus were still preventing access in Italy.'

There they stood, in the car park: Patrick, Agna, and Oumi.

'Well,' says Patrick. 'You just stand there.'

Only the team doctor was allowed inside, and that was José Ibarguren. 'We call him *Doki*, little doctor, because he's not that tall,' says Patrick.

It was then a case of waiting.
And waiting.
And waiting.
'Endless waiting,' says Patrick.
'There we stood, in the car park. The press arrived, the first journalists on the scene.' Once again he repeats: 'We couldn't go inside.'

Then there was a new phone call: from Remco himself, calling from his bed, barely a few dozen metres away inside the hospital. Patrick, Agna, and Oumi all reacted in their own way. Still tender in years, Oumi was all emotion, heart-rending, moving emotion. So was Patrick. What had been bubbling up inside him, what he had suppressed, he finally gave free rein to – emotions can do that to a man. All of that wanted to come out in Agna too, but at times like these she becomes the epitome of calm: she kept calm, as probably only mothers can. Agna wanted to be there for Remco, she wanted to look after her son. 'A mother can start to panic as well. Of course she can! But she can keep calm and she does that perfectly.'

And so Agna listened coolly and calmly to what Remco had to say. She listened to the bad news: Remco was in a lot of trouble. She listened as he said that fractures had been found in his femur and coccyx. This was serious, concerning news. Remco had to go up to the operating theatre – immediately! His artery had suddenly started bleeding and needed to be cauterised at once. Fortunately, the intervention was successful. But the team doctors concluded that other operations were not possible in Bergamo. They wanted to have Remco treated in Herentals by Toon Claes – cycling enthusiast, admirer, and climber of the legendary Mont Ventoux. The surgeon is world-renowned, knows the sport of cycling inside out, and can assess injuries perfectly. Remco would be in good hands there.

Meanwhile in Como, Jakob Fuglsang had won the tour in a time of 5 hours, 32 minutes and 54 seconds. He beat George Bennett by 31 seconds and Aleksandr Vlasov by 51 seconds. Bauke Mollema finished fourth, Giulio Ciccone fifth, and Vincenzo Nibali sixth – the leading group had maintained its lead.

'The team insisted that we visit them at their hotel in the evening,' Patrick continued. 'They wanted us to eat something together with them. The boys sat there deflated, the atmosphere was heavy. They still didn't know what condition Remco was in. But then Agna filled them in on all the details.'

Any idea of Remco being able to board the plane the next day was ruled out because of not knowing how his lungs and overall condition might react to the pressurised atmosphere. No, they couldn't take that risk. 'I dropped Agna and Oumi off at the airport and I stayed behind in Bergamo.' That was a difficult moment for Agna, finally leaving her son behind in Italy, as it also was for Oumi, who was leaving her beloved partner behind. Or rather, no, that's not actually how to look at it: it wasn't that way at all. Agna and Oumi flew home so they could be there already when Remco was allowed to return to Belgium. Agna and Oumi were being pragmatic – as soon as he was able, Remco could return to his own safe and familiar home environment.

In the end, Patrick was finally allowed into the hospital. He saw that coronavirus was still very much in evidence. There were rows of beds in the corridors, people were connected up to equipment, with drips and tubes and masks everywhere. The virus had still not gone from here and it would cause new misery later in the year. The pandemic was still wreaking havoc. Patrick had to put on a protective suit and be disinfected. No risks could be taken on the way to the Intensive Care Unit where Remco was. Finally, Patrick was allowed into the ward. There he saw his son, affected by pain and medication.

As soon as Patrick entered the ward, Remco sat upright in bed. He looked at his father and began to chat.

'The Giro, papa! The Giro, it's going to be OK,' said Remco.
'I have to be ready for the Giro d'Italia.'
'All in good time,' said Patrick.
'The Giro,' said Remco.
'There's always next year,' replied Patrick.
'No,' said Remco.
'No! This year!'
'No! This year, in October!'
'We'll see,' said Patrick.
'We'll see.'

Patrick resolved to stay as long as he could with Remco in the ward. Because as soon he were to leave the ward, he might not be let back in on account of the coronavirus measures. Afterwards, friends Pascal and Joeri De Knop sat and waited for news in the hospital's reception area.

That news came, and once again, it was not good: Remco would have to stay for another two days. Flying was still not an option. That would eventually be possible 48 hours later. 'That was in a special plane on a special stretcher. Remco was secured in a special enclosure,' says Patrick. He scrolls back through his photos and his voice chokes again: 'Look,' he points. He pauses, swallows, and then continues: 'That's when Remco himself realised how badly he'd been hurt. Only then did it hit home for real.'

Remco was sedated before the plane took off...

'Well,' says Patrick. 'It was no longer about the Tour of Lombardy and who was in the leading group. It was no longer about who would be the fastest in the sprint or who would be the favourite in the Giro.'

Patrick falls silent for a moment again.
'It was no longer about a cyclist. Now it was about our child. Now it was about our child who needed us.'

'Our child in need.'

Then began the long recovery. Firstly in Herentals, where Remco was operated on. There are photos of when Remco was able to take his first steps again. 'Ten steps, that's how many he managed the first time. Then, of course, we thought: wow, Remco can do that already! But when I reflect on those images, he looked so frail then. Just look, how fragile he was.'

Then there was a particularly difficult period: Remco lay in bed, experiencing pain, he could get up for a moment, but then had to lie back down. A bed was put up in the living room of Agna and Patrick's home. Oumi took care of her boyfriend while simultaneously studying upstairs – this was an unusual situation for a boy and a girl who were so young and should have been busy with other things. It was a period of juggling schedules and appointments: the two parents left for work early in the morning – the men at the sites don't wait and neither do the customers at the hairdressing salon. That's just how life was then.

Patrick pauses to think and then continues: 'Of course, Remco knew that we were always there for him, that's what parents are for. But from an early age, Remco had learned to make his own plans. As a young boy, he saw how we were always kept busy because we were self-employed.' Patrick recounts the story of his own dramatic fall when he was a plasterer standing on a scaffold and suddenly fell off. Agna only arrived at the hospital's emergency department that evening. She couldn't just abandon her own clients during the day and she made sure that the orders continued to be processed and that invoices were created and paid. Patrick remained in hospital for seven months – such experiences toughen a person. 'Remco was eight years old at the time,' says Patrick. 'It impacted heavily on him but he never let it get him down.'

At that time, while still a small child, Remco was the strong person he is now.

Back to Remco's recovery, back to August 2020.

'That was all extremely significant,' says Patrick.

And once again, Agna sensed perfectly what was happening. Again, she saw that something wasn't right: it wasn't Remco lying there anymore, Agna saw that in his look. He was heavily sedated, too heavily probably. Remco's eyes appeared to have turned grey, his body was giving off alarm signals and going into shock. He was becoming a shadow of himself before their very eyes. The medication, the painkillers, were reduced. Very quickly, Remco felt a lot better. He regained his strength and on 12 September – barely a month after the accident – he was already back on the rollers. Straight away he was ready to set new targets.

2020 was a particularly heavy year. The year of the severe setback.
'No,' says Patrick.
'No, life isn't always a bed of roses.
Life can be hard, too.'
Even so, he says...

'Even so, the 15th of August 2020 was a lucky day for us.'
'Let's not forget.'
'Our child was still with us.'
'Remco was still alive.'
'Remco lives on.'

'Other parents haven't been so lucky.'

Patrick then goes on to talk about Wouter Weylandt, about Bjorg Lambrecht and Gino Mäder, young riders in the prime of their lives who fell in a race and never got up again – young riders who lost the promise of a wonderful life forever. About his best friend, Danny Alaerts. In 1991, Danny and Patrick had just signed a contract with the professional team of Histor and the two best friends were about to make the following year a fantastic one. But it wasn't to be: on 7 October 1991, Danny fell during the race in Haacht, having hit the tow bar of a caravan parked on the side of the road. That evening, Danny passed away and remained a 23-year-old forever. 'I carry his photo with me always in my wallet. I'll never forget Danny,' says Patrick.

He talks about Stef Loos, Remco's best friend. On Sunday, 17 March 2019, Stef was taking part in a race in Tournai. Suddenly, Stef, along with a bunch of other riders, went off course. There were no more marshals, and cars from normal traffic were coming towards them. A van collided with Stef at a crossroads. Stef passed away the next day, a 19-year-old forever. Remco lost his friend, his best mate. 'We still have his keychain. We'll never forget Stef,' says Patrick.

Patrick falls silent for some time. A tear falls.

'Let's not forget that', he repeats.
'Our child is still with us.'
'We were lucky.'

In 2022, Remco won the road race at the UCI Road World Championships in Wollongong, Australia.

In 2023, Remco won the time trial at the UCI Road World Championships in Stirling, Scotland.

In 2024, Remco won gold in the time trial at the Paris Olympics.

In 2024, Remco won gold in the road race at the Paris Olympics.

2

THIS IS THE

It's the story of a young man, who at the age of 24 has catapulted himself to the top of international cycling in a very short time. It's a story that takes your breath away – how can someone so young achieve so much? How is it possible for a rider to win so much? This is the story of genes and DNA and of all that strength that is the source of talent.

It's the story of a father who looked on wide-eyed at what his son did while he was still a footballer. It's those moments that the father will never forget because most, if not all, have something to say about his son's character. This is the story of two points in time when Remco decided on his own future, firstly when he was still a youth of 12 and secondly when reached the age of 15. These were the times when Patrick Evenepoel realised that Remco was going to be somebody. He can still vividly recall them.

The first time was when his son was 12 years old. The young lad then told his parents that he was fed up with travelling back and forth as a junior footballer for PSV and that it would be best if he could go and live with a host family in Eindhoven. There you stand. As parents who are handing over their only child.

The other instance was when Remco was at the conference table at Anderlecht, Belgium's top football club, and decided that it would be better for him to get out of his contract. There they sat, the members of the board and father Patrick, stunned by such brazen audacity. Remco got up, shook hands with the football club's top brass, looked them in the eyes briefly, and quit. In his head, he'd decided that he needed to map out his own life, as a *wunderkind* does at that age. Did he already know, perhaps, what was going to happen in fewer than ten years – in 2024?

This is story of ups and downs.

It's the story of powerful dynamos who amuse themselves on training rides in Spain. Of live wires with an excess of energy, who can be even harder on themselves when it matters, even harder so as to get even better – young men like Tadej Pogačar, Mathieu van der Poel, and Wout van Aert. And Remco.

This is the story of three standout weeks in France in the summer of 2024. It's the story of three weeks in France that, crazily enough, began in Italy on 29 June, with a first stage in the Tour de France from Florence to Rimini – the start of the Tour in the boot of Italy, full of expectation and hope, ambition and tension: how would Remco fare in the Tour de France, and what could people expect from him? This is the story of success in those three weeks in France – Remco had done what people were hoping for.

This is the story that plays out on Saturday, 27 July 2024, a golden day that began at 17:22 in the early evening, in the rain, right in the heart of Paris, on ultra-slippery roads. It was day one of the Olympic Games, everything still lay ahead for the athletes, for all the men and women who had spent years preparing for their moment of truth – who could predict what might happen there in the shadow of the Eiffel Tower? It's the story that became a march of triumph for the main character in this book that lasted 36 minutes, 12 seconds, and 26 one-hundredths. Then he put his hand up high and was Olympic Champion in the cycling time trial.

It's a story that belongs to a young man and a young woman who are building a life together.

This is the story of Saturday, 3 August, the day on which the Olympic Games entered their second week, along Montmartre and the Moulin Rouge, through the streets of Paris, past thousands, tens of thousands of people, exuberantly waving flags and eager to cheer and shout, propelling the riders forward in the road race, with Wout van Aert, Jasper Stuyven, and Tiesj Benoot slowing down, breaking away at 15.1 kilometres from the finish, where on the left side of the road stands the sign, it's actually true – only 15 kilometres to go, looking back, away from the rest, into history, with the number 6 emblazoned on his back, wearing a red helmet and a yellow-blue jersey. Thirteen kilometres to go still, shouting to the man on the motorcycle: 'Don't get too close!' Through the bend, left, right, still 12.2 kilometres left and already a 19-second lead over Valentin Madouas, with the others straggling even further behind. This is the story of an Olympic exploit, the second one in just under a week. It's the story of the head and the legs – who can explain how you maintain focus, barely seven days after the first great triumph? This is the story of the bike and the flat tyre at 3.8 kilometres, of the arm in the air, of jumping off and shouting: 'Bike! 'Bike! Bike! (Check out the images, they do exist.) And waiting, but only for a few seconds, and there it is, the new bike, and then on our way again. The lead is steady at one minute, over there through the gate, along the Seine and then smiling at the camera, with eyes full of wonder, shaking with his right hand, like someone does when they have just got hot, too hot – 'What just happened to me?' And there's the arch, the triumphal arch, and then the bike can be held up high in the air, and soon to follow is the podium and the two gold medals – what a fantastic idea of Oumi's to bring that first gold medal to the ceremony. This is the story of the rider who astonished the world.

This is the story of the author who visited many people's homes where he was warmly welcomed, who had a coffee while he listened to tales full of love, wonder, and admiration. When asked whether they had seen it coming that this young man would build such a career, have such a will to succeed, so much ambition, from one and all the answer was always: yes! The people in this story offer a glimpse behind the curtain, each from their own perspective, their own viewpoints – the stories they tell come from the heart of the peloton, from the heart of the family.

This is the story of in-depth conversations with Remco himself – giving you, the reader, a front seat from which you'll get to know the young man, the sportsman, better.

Hoping you enjoy it.

3

'LADS WHO ARE NOT YET MATURE CAN BE THE MOST TALENTED.'

Kevin De Weert was a strong rider.

Between 2003 and 2015 he rode professionally for Rabobank, Quick Step-Innergetic, Cofidis, Quick Step again, Omega Pharma-Quick Step, and Team Lotto NL-Jumbo. Top teams, one and all. Kevin was no winner, but that didn't matter. He was simply a useful rider who knew his place in the peloton and one who achieved his best results in the Tour de France. In 2010, he finished eighteenth in the overall classification – although that was ultimately changed officially to sixteenth after Alberto Contador and Denis Menchov were disqualified due to doping issues. A year later, Kevin was thirteenth, but after the disqualification of – once again – Contador, that became twelfth. 'During the Tour, I never had a really bad day,' he recounts. 'And that gets you a long way.'

In the 2013 Tour of Spain, De Weert had a serious fall. After that, he never got back to a decent level. 'I'd signed a contract with Jumbo, but no, it wasn't working for me any more.' Halfway through 2015, he called it quits – that was on 27 May, the day of his birthday. Kevin was then 33 years old. Something remarkable had happened during all those years. De Weert was quite often selected for the elite world championships. 'I took part five years in a row,' he recounts. Kevin De Weert was seen as the man who propelled the team, kept it together, and slowed down when necessary – he was the man who established the strategy during the race.

Jos Smets, sports director at Belgian Cycling (the Belgian Cycling Federation, if you will), saw potential in a collaboration with De Weert – Smets knew even before anyone from the newspapers, magazines, radio, or television that Kevin would stop racing. As far as Jos was concerned, he could join the Cycling Federation. The only problem was: there was no position available in May, nor was there any budget. So it would have to wait until September 2015. Waiting that long wasn't a problem for Kevin De Weert, and in September he became development coach for the Belgian national team. His task: to set up the so-called climb project.

'We got started on the climb project with the juniors,' recounts Kevin. It should be no surprise that this happened with this youth category: 'Some riders are already quite mature, while others still need to develop and haven't actually finished growing yet. And then you see what happens in the typical races around the church tower: those who are not fully grown yet are mercilessly outridden by the boys who have already experienced a growth spurt.' And that is precisely the problem, says De Weert: 'Those *lads* who are not yet mature may well have the most talent. It's then just a case of scouting for them, discovering them and motivating them with a training camp, *little by little*. We don't want to lose those lads.'

So that was how the climb project came about: juniors who remained under the radar, who were not to be found in the results of the Saturday and Sunday races, could register via a form on the national team's website. When registering, they were asked for two things: a motivational letter – why did they think they might be able to climb? And a fitness test, which would show whether such a young rider – 'Perhaps only weighing 45 kilograms', says Kevin – could put out some serious wattage. He talks enthusiastically about the project – 'It was all managed very nicely' – and mentions that sometimes the weirdest things appeared in the motivational letters: 'I want to make a lot of money' or 'I want to get rich through cycling'. Sometimes you got to read heartwarming, touching sentences: 'Last summer me and my dad went to the Vosges and we climbed the mountains together, side by side. I got to know my dad better. I enjoyed that.'

Kevin explains that the youngsters could register from early March until sometime in May, and that at least a hundred young riders had done so. 'Me and Erwin Koninckx, the national cycling team's exercise physiologist, read through all those forms. We selected about 30 candidates from the 100 applications. They received an invitation from us to a training camp in La Gleize, in the Ardennes.'

So there they were, the young cyclists, ready for a 70-kilometre ride, with a 5-minute test on the Côte de la Brume near Trois-Ponts. There, by way of a benchmark, Koninckx had chosen a 2.6-kilometre stretch with a 6% incline – ideal for testing endurance climbing ability. This was followed by a 1-minute test on the Côte de Wanne over 450 metres with a 10% incline – ideal for testing explosive climbing ability. We measured wattages, took blood, and in the evening – over a tasty, healthy pasta – we analysed the results. We narrowed the 30 down to 5 who were allowed to join a new training camp, this time in the Vosges. The 5 would meet another 5 juniors in France, who had already won races, were already strong and known to the Federation. In the Vosges, they would be tested on the Ballon d'Alsace, a legendary mountain pass.

Kevin sums up: 'That was the format of the climb project. What about the names it produced? Maxim Van Gils, for instance. Or Harm Vanhoucke. And Ilan Van Wilder.'

Kevin De Weert pauses for a moment, sips his coffee and says: 'And then Remco came into the picture.'

4

'WHEN I READ
THAT, I SAID TO
MYSELF: WOW!
THAT MUST BE
SOME CHARACTER!
HE WAS SIMPLY
THE BOSS AMONG
ALL THOSE EGOS.'

In 2017, registrations for that year's climb project had already closed. Again, 30 riders would be selected, from which five young men would be allowed to go to the Vosges. That was all completely clear. But a day after the deadline, Kevin De Weert got another email: It said: 'Dear Coach Kevin, can my son still register?' Plus: 'I realise we are too late.' Sender: Patrick Evenepoel. Kevin clicked open the motivation letter – it was a long, pleasant text. Patrick talked about his son Remco, about his career as a footballer with Anderlecht, PSV, KV Mechelen, and the Rode Duivels. About how his son had been the captain of various teams and about his drive. But Patrick also wrote that his son no longer wanted to play football and had set his sights on cycling: Remco wanted to become a cyclist.

'I read that last,' says De Weert. 'And I said to myself: 'Wow! This chap is 16 years old and he's captain of the Rode Duivels! Footballers are all ego, and he's their captain? He's got to be some character!' De Weert also opened the file with the enclosed fitness test. Something was off here, which Kevin noticed immediately: this wasn't a cycling test, it was a running test. 'It goes without saying, that wasn't the information we were after,' says he. 'A running test!'
But so be it, thought De Weert, one rider more or one less. What difference did it make? Not that much, really? One extra lad? Why not? And so for the climb project, they confirmed Remco Evenepoel – the footballer – could go to La Gleize.

One thing struck him immediately there in the Ardennes: 'On meeting, Remco addressed me as "coach", not as "Kevin" or something else. I was really struck by that. If I reflect on it now, it can hardly be anything other than that Remco's attitude was connected with the fact that he was coming from football. A footballer is actually already an adult at the age of 16. At that age, many are already ready to train or play with the youth team and even the first eleven. Remco had that look about him, that mature attitude of an adult. Remco wasn't a child any more.'

'Anyway', says Kevin, 'we did the test in the Ardennes. None of the other young riders knew Remco or had any idea who he was. He wasn't affiliated to a club, he was just there with a bike provided by his father. The footballer had yet to ride in any race.'

Remco's results were respectable. But no more than that: 'Remco was average, somewhere just beyond fifth place,' De Weert continues. Or in other words: 'Numerically, Remco was actually not selected for the Vosges.' The explanation? Simple: 'With a strongly developed upper body, Remco looked like a footballer, like someone who did contact sports. But riders don't need that, for them it's better to have minimal upper body.'

In the evening, while we were having pasta, Remco came up to Kevin. 'Well, coach? How were my tests? What are the results? Were they good, coach?'

Again, Kevin thought: *well, I never*, this lad has the kind of drive you don't often come across. And so he made a decision again – intuitively: Remco could go to the Vosges. Once more, the same thing happened as in the Ardennes: Remco's results were respectable, but no more than that. To quote Kevin: 'The results were good, but nothing outstanding.'

Kevin De Weert and Erwin Koninckx reviewed Remco's results together again and were still amazed by the wattages that the young man could already push out. When they put all his numbers under the microscope, they had to ask themselves this question: could this ex-footballer be a diamond in the rough? Might Remco Evenepoel have the ability to become a rider?

During the evening, after the plate of spaghetti, Kevin and Erwin called Remco over. They wanted to tell him something: 'Look,' said Erwin, 'those are the wattages you're pushing out. They're not bad at all.' Remco looked at the results. Erwin carried on: 'If you were to lose 8 kilograms from your upper body, then your riding would be up at the top in the current database of the tables.' Erwin repeated what he'd just said: 'If you lose 8 kilograms from your upper body, then...Yeah.'

Remco took the comments on board, went to Sporting Anderlecht's nutrition coach for targeted advice, contacted Energy Lab for testing and scientific analyses, and visited the Bakala Academy. It was founded by Zdenek Bakala, the businessman born in the Czech Republic who is obsessed with cycling and its development, the same person who has been financially steering the team(s) of manager Patrick Lefevere for many years. If Remco was going to go for it, it was vital that he started doing different training. After all, he wasn't a footballer anymore. In cycling, good abdominal and back muscles are quintessential. Putting it somewhat more crudely: 'he's got to become as slight as possible up top and as heavy as possible down below,' recounts Kevin de Weert.

As a training objective, this was a hard nut to crack. But when Remco reported back for a training camp a few months later, he was 8 kilograms lighter in the right place: his upper body.

'And the rest is history,' says Kevin.
Remco had become a cyclist; he was now a first-year junior.

In his first real competition in a peloton, he finished 71st; by the end of his first season, he had already won seven races. At the World Championship held in mid-September 2017 in Bergen (Norway), Remco was the team leader – even then. These were the winners: Peter Sagan in the road race for the pros; Tom Dumoulin in the time trial. In the road race for the under-23 riders, Benoît Cosnefroy won, and in the time trial, it was Mikkel Bjerg. In the juniors, it was Julius Johansen, and in the time trial, it was Tom Pidcock.

'I was there too,' Kevin says with a laugh. 'I'll never forget it. Remco was already so good in his first half-year that he was indeed the team leader.

The junior team's national coach had told him that at the meeting the day before the race. A bit later on there was a knock at my hotel door.'

Kevin De Weert opened the door of his room. Remco was standing there. He says: 'I've just heard that I'm team leader. What do I have to do now? Kevin answered: 'Keep an eye on the better riders. If you still have some juice left in your legs at the end, you can try something.'

But, says Kevin: 'Remco didn't ride that world championship to the end. He'd fallen.'

The fact that Remco had fallen in that race was not really news. In the few months since he'd become a rider, he'd done that quite often. 'Yes,' says Kevin De Weert, 'how did that happen? Simple: he had missed out on the first principles of riding in a peloton. He'd never ridden in a peloton before, he couldn't steer. Really? You have to imbibe that from a young age, riding in a peloton. Remco had missed out on those first years in racing, between the ages of 14 and 16. That haunted him for a long time. Remco fell a lot, an awful lot.

During his second world championship, in Innsbruck (Austria) in 2018, Remco fell yet again. But no matter: he got back up, rode away from the rest, and won with a lead of 1'25" over the German Marius Mayrhofer and 1'36" over the Italian Alessandro Fancellu. Remco also became world champion in the time trial – Australian Lucas Plapp and Italian Andrea Piccolo followed one-and-a-half minutes behind (Ilan Van Wilder finished sixth).

Kevin De Weert: 'Just as soon as he dropped those 8 kilograms, Remco was phenomenal.'

And the falling? His place in the peloton that Remco wasn't yet able to find properly? The young rider solved that in his own inimical way: he would ride ahead of the peloton, escaping quickly and early, often right from the very start. Honestly? He did that practically all the time, alone at the front, pushing ahead, pedalling, he was that good – away from the rest. In 2018, Remco became European champion on the road with a lead of 9'44" over the Swiss Alexandre Balmer and 9 minutes and 46 seconds over the Spaniard Carlos Rodriguez and Ilan Van Wilder. In the time trial, Remco finished ahead of Ilan Van Wilder and the Italian Antonio Tiberi.

Kevin repeats once again: 'Remco was a phenomenon.'

After the climb project, De Weert and Erwin Koninckx had done their job of turning the former footballer into a full-fledged cyclist. Remco moved to Forte, one of the top teams in 2017 in terms of support for newcomers, juniors, and under-23 riders.

5

'DO YOU HAVE A
SPARE JERSEY
LAYING AROUND?
OUR REMCO NEEDS
A RACE KIT.'

'I got a phone call one day,' says Patrick Verschueren.

From 1984 to 1992, Patrick Verschueren was a professional cyclist. He started with Safir, the team of the Aalst brewery, which enjoyed its heyday during the carnival of the East Flemish city until it was taken over by the global AB Inbev and – eventually – disappeared. Safir was the sponsor of a cycling team filled with good riders from 1978 to 1988, who made a name for themselves in regional races and competitions just below the highest level. Between 1978 and 1988, riders like Werner Devos, Ronny Van Holen – who was even world champion in the juniors – Dirk Heirweg, Luc Colyn, Eddy Vanhaerens, and Etienne De Wilde accomplished great things for the team. Men who, after a fantastic career, were past their prime, won stages in the Tour of Spain (Michel Pollentier) and Bordeaux-Paris (Herman Vanspringel). In short: Safir – along with several co-sponsors over the years – was a great team that contributed to the atmosphere of cycling in the 1980s.

Patrick Verschueren had debuted in this team when he was 22. 'After two years, I moved to Roland-Skala in 1986, a team with quite a few strong riders, such as Hennie Kuiper, Jesper Skibby, Brian Holm, Herman Frison, and Johan Capiot. A solid level, you know.' Patrick didn't do badly, not at all badly – he could even have moved to Panasonic and Superconfex, top teams at that time. 'But I opted for Lotto, in Belgium. Why? The financial picture! Don't you know?' Patrick rode in the Tour de France four times – 'I was once third in a stage, and that was at the start of the Tour. If I'd won, I would have had the yellow jersey. But, yeah.' At Lotto, he was a super domestique, these are Patrick's own words. He rode for Johan Museeuw, Johan Bruyneel, and Claude Cricquielion. 'I was highly valued, I was the guy who could create echelons and I held my own for a long time in races like Paris-Nice.' Verschueren says it again, he really wants to emphasize this: 'Yes, I was valued. I never had to beg to get a contract.' In 1992 he personally decided to quit – 'Mind you,' he says, 'I could still have signed new contracts, the teams weren't fed up with me yet, I could still do it.' After his career in cycling, Patrick

Verschueren did 'this and that in regular life, working on bikes and such'. But the siren call of the cycling life on the road soon called again – once in the race, always in the race. He started coaching novices and juniors who were already promising young riders. 'One of them was Danny van de Tuurk,' Patrick recalls. 'He was a Dutchman, a young man with grit. I let him start off in Prins der Nieuwelingen. One day, Danny told me that his dad dealt in cycling clothing. I heard him out. Out of politeness, after all there are a lot of people who deal in clothing.' Danny's father – Bert by name – had a business in Groningen. 'I drove up there then,' says Verschueren. 'It was a considerable distance, over 400 kilometres. Coming from Flanders, you can't get there *one-two-three*, just like that.

But never mind, all those kilometres northwards turned out to be worth it: Bert asked if Patrick could set up a Belgian branch of his clothing line. Forte België was born.

And then Verschueren received that phone call.

'It was Patrick Evenepoel hanging on the line.'
'Patrick,' says the other Patrick, 'our Remco needs a race kit because he's entered for a time trial on Sunday. Do you have anything lying around?' he asked. 'No problem,' Patrick, the man of the jerseys, replied to Patrick, the father of the budding cyclist. 'I'll bring the kit myself on Sunday. And I'll fit *handlebars* to *his bike*.' You know what I mean, for sure, Patrick Verschueren explains now: 'Handlebars specially designed for riding time trials.' Patrick still vividly remembers that Sunday. 'Our Remco wants to race,' Patrick Evenepoel had impressed upon him. 'And he's quit football.' That's all well and good, thought Patrick Verschueren, and – he had to admit – he'd heard the stories about the footballer who had participated in Kevin De Weert's climb project and he'd even chatted with Kevin about that young man. But Forte, which supported Verschueren's team as a sponsor, was a strong team; they raced all the major competitions for juniors, all over the place, in Spain, Italy, and

France. And they won a lot. In other words: was there now a place for someone who had not yet ridden in any race whatsoever?

That Sunday of the time trial, Fred Vandervennet was also in attendance.

Back in the 1980s, Fred had been an excellent marathon runner, having become Belgian champion in long-distance running three times. In 2017, he'd been a coach for quite a while. One of his disciples: Remco Evenepoel. 'That chap, he's a star,' Fred had said to Patrick Verschueren when they had struck up a conversation. 'What that boy can do, I've never experienced before. That pedal cadence, his capacity. Unbelievable.' Fred had taken his leave of Verschueren, had glanced back for a moment, waved, and had got behind the wheel of his Ford Kuga. He was going to follow Remco in his very first race.

6

'I WAS SAT AT THE
KITCHEN TABLE.
THAT BOY WAS
RUNNING AROUND
WITH A BALL.
JUST PLAYING
AND DRIBBLING.
I THOUGHT: WHAT
IS THAT? WHAT'S
HE DOING?'

The story of Fred Vandervennet and Remco began way before that Sunday in 2017. And that story is deserving of a prominent place here. Fred is now in his seventies, but his passion for movement and his knowledge of sports science have remained completely intact. Fred Vandervennet still knows how to intensively prepare an athlete for great things. If they ask him, he still coaches young lads – 'Look,' he says, as he draws up training plans on paper, with a pencil. 'That's what they get from me. If I've heard nothing from them over the next three weeks or so, then I leave them in peace. They have to come to me, I'm not going to run after them.'

Fred's story deserves a prominent place, of course, because he had a front row seat when young Remco was already showing his potential. That was on the day Fred visited the young couple Agna and Patrick Evenepoel.

We need to take a moment, dear reader, to set the stage for the moment that will unfold at Agna and Patrick's kitchen table. Fred settles in comfortably with a coffee at his home in Diest-Molenstede. Vino the dog is laying at his feet. Fred's wife, Mia, has retreated to her sewing studio. Fred and Mia got married 50 years ago, so she's heard it all before.

Fred recounts how he was approached by the bosses of Histor, a paint manufacturer and sponsor of the cycling team Histor-Sigma, to provide training for the riders. In itself, that was pretty revolutionary in the 1980s: a coach working with schedules and detailed plans, not something you'd come across in many teams around then. 'I developed my training sessions based on three important principles. Principle number one: train specifically. In other words, runners must run, swimmers must swim, and cyclists must cycle. Principle number two: train intensively and fast. That means you gradually cover a distance faster and faster. It doesn't make sense to increase the distance while maintaining the same intensity. It's better to stick to the distance but cover it increasingly faster, harder, more intensively. Principle number three: ensure variation, e.g. don't train over the same course all the time, mix it up.' Fred drew that know-how not only from his own career as a marathon runner but also from his degree in Physical Education (now a Master's) from KU Leuven. He'd been an excellent student there and simultaneously served as a sounding board for Professor of Exercise Physiology Bart Van den Eynde and athletics coach Mon Vanden Eynde – the man who had success with Gaston Roelants, Miel Puttemans, and Ivo Van Damme, sporting greats one and all. Fred sums up: 'I know about training.'

Fred needs to take a brief detour here to get to the essence of his story later on. 'One day, I got a visit from the people at Histor-Sigma. But they said that they didn't want to take me on just as an in-house trainer. They also wanted me as a manager for their companies.' Fred laughs: no, he didn't know anything about paint or wallpaper, apart from the fact that the latter was sold in rolls. The owners didn't think the lack of knowledge was a big deal: Fred received an education into the wonderful world of interior decorating. What kind of education, exactly? Fred was given a book with all the ins and outs of paint and wallpaper, and a room on the first floor of the premises that Histor-Sigma had recently taken over: Mommaerts in Diest. Although Fred still wasn't completely au fait with the products in the company, he was good with figures – that was the scientist in him. 'And those figures weren't good,' he admits. 'There were too many staff for too small a turnover. So I had to take measures, let people go. I did something unusual for those days. I let the older employees go and held on to the younger ones – after all, they had small children and a mortgage to pay. They're still grateful to me for that.' Later on, Histor-Sigma expanded and relocated the business to Hasselt. Fred Vandervennet was now in charge of two companies. Or putting it another way: Fred was more manager than coach – more a seller of paints, varnishes and associated products than sports coach for a cycling team. 'And yet I visited those cyclists at home,' he says. 'All of them received a plan from me, a schedule for the next year. After the season, for example, I required them to start training again in November. No, taking three months off simply wasn't on. No, they weren't allowed to put on 10 kilograms. That wasn't how I worked. People were amused by that approach, that I do know. Franky Van Oyen, one of our riders, was good friends with Eddy Planckaert. When Franky told Eddy just before Christmas that he was already hard at it, Eddy found that rather odd. He only got back on his bike on New Year's Day.'

The men from Histor-Sigma won the E3 Prize in Harelbeke in the spring of 1990 with Søren Lilholt, and Gent-Wevelgem with Herman Frison. In 1988, Etienne De Wilde became the Belgian champion, and in 1991, Benjamin Van Itterbeeck followed in his footsteps. Wilfried Peeters, Brian Holm, and – towards the tail end of their impressive careers – Hennie Kuiper (world champion in 1975!) and Lucien Van Impe (Tour winner in 1976!) rode for the team. In short: Fred Vandervennet's approach was vindicated: 'I was a pioneer,' he says with pride and satisfaction. 'I was also training many talented youngster back then, men with a VO2 max of 80. Those are serious readings. I had those riders tested by Professor Bart Van den Eynde because I saw their potential.' Fred Vandervennet did his best to bring those young riders into the team. He discussed them with Sports Director Willy Teirlinck. Names included Wim Sels, Patrick De Wael, Kurt Huyghe, Danny Alaerts.

And Patrick Evenepoel.

One day in 1993, Fred was sitting in front of the television, watching the GP de Wallonie. 'Hey,' Fred muttered to himself, and peered more closely at the screen. 'Is that...? Aren't I training him? Yes, that really is him!' That was the day on which Patrick Evenepoel won the sweetest race of his short career. Three days earlier, he'd been 113th in the Tour of Spain – Tony Rominger won the Vuelta. In the two days between Spain and Wallonie, Patrick spent hours behind the motorbike, cycling away his fatigue in super-compensation and preparing for his feat, there in the vicinity of the Citadel of Namur, on 20 May 1993. That's character, *n'est pas*? 'Patrick wasn't a professional cyclist for very long,' says Fred. 'He suffered too much from allergies. Pity.' But Patrick and Fred stayed in touch. Vandervennet attended Patrick and Agna's wedding, and he was sent a birth announcement card when their son – Remco, was born in January 2000.

'And then, several years later, I went to visit the young couple and sat around their kitchen table. At the time, the young boy was still small, his head barely reaching the edge of the table.' The kid was playing with a ball, an image that Fred will never forget. And that little boy kept right on playing with that ball, around the table, under the table, an impressive demonstration of coordination between eye and foot by Remco. 'That was something I'd never seen before.'

Time went by, the years passed, and Fred got a call – it was from Patrick Evenepoel. 'They've taken him on! Anderlecht has taken him on,' said Patrick. That sounded very promising, there might be a future as a footballer ahead for young Remco. Of course, you already know that he became a cyclist, but it's good to recall some memories that characterise what happened after Remco arrived at Anderlecht.

For example, Fred Vandervennet accompanied Patrick and Agna to the youth complex in Neerpede several times, seeing there that Remco could become an extremely good centre midfielder – 'a slow Zinedine Zidane', Fred says about that now. But he also saw that Remco was often placed as left back, a position that didn't suit him. And Fred noticed that Remco was annoyed about that. Later, Fred also went to watch PSV a few times and saw how Remco got a yellow card, then started arguing with the referee, and three minutes later got a red card – he'd been on the field for fewer than 10 minutes. Remco's temperament was to blame is how Fred sees it now. 'Then he started to grumble at the referee. He couldn't tolerate that he'd been given a reprimand, one that he felt was unfair.' And, Fred goes on to add: 'He thought the red card was so unfair, that the referee had beaten him. Then he came crying on my shoulder. No, Remco doesn't like losing.'

In any case, something had happened at Anderlecht and PSV. Remco was a bit too slow. And he wanted to work on that. Fred had to help him with training schedules that he could take with him when he went on holiday with the family. 'He wanted to be faster,' Remco had told Fred (and his father Patrick). Fred could certainly help him with that, give him some coaching. Only: 'There are limits to how much faster you can make someone,' recounts the coach now. He explains it in terms of muscle function, using his own words: 'If you don't have enough white fibres in your muscles, it's not possible to increase your speed significantly. After all, those white fibres are precisely what support speed. Whether or not you have a lot of those fibres is down to genetics. Some athletes have more white fibres than others, that's just the way it is. The red fibres on the other hand are what are referred to as endurance fibres. But something remarkable happens in the muscles: if you train a lot for endurance, the white fibres also become endurance fibres. The reverse is not true: training a lot for speed doesn't mean that the red fibres will become fast fibres. In short: if you don't have enough white fibres in your muscles, you can work as hard as you want at becoming really fast, but it won't work completely.' When Fred applies this theory, this science, to today's cycling heroes, the men who want (and are able) to win major tours, then this is how he assesses what they can achieve in terms of reaching the top of a mountain pass: Tadej Pogačar is extremely explosive and can wait a long time before he starts sprinting – his speed is certainly extremely high. He is like a spring that – hop, hop, hop – suddenly accelerates away. Primož Roglič needs more time and is best off attacking one kilometre from the top. And Remco? 'It's best for him to attack from even further away,' Fred says. After all, the tests have indicated that he doesn't have as many white muscle fibres. But, says Fred: 'Remco will keep on improving year on year. He'll still get stronger up until his 27th birthday. And, really important: Remco is a worker. A hard worker. And, even more important: Remco masters the game. There's a head on that body of his.'

'Shouldn't we test him sometime?' Patrick Evenepoel had asked Fred Vandervennet when they were on their way to a football match in which Remco was playing. 'Can't we put him on the treadmill sometime?' Fred concurred, and he still remembers exactly how it went. 'So I put Remco on the treadmill, while accompanied by Peter Hespel, also an exercise physiologist and professor in Leuven. Little by little, I turned the tread-mill up faster and faster until we got to 18 kilometres per hour.'

Hespel looked at Vandervennet: 'What??'

'You should know,' Fred says now, 'that 18 kilometres per hour is fast. Then you're a genuine athlete. Note that Remco was still just 17 years old. And a footballer! He was a *striker!*' The test was progressive, in blocks of 8 minutes, with the speed gradually increasing. How long can some-one maintain such a test? Simple: Until they stop the clock, until they indicate that it's enough. Or: 'Until you're dead on your feet,' as Fred Vandervennet puts it.

Professor Hespel had looked at Fred again, saying: 'This lad, he's so ca-pable.'

But Fred and Patrick weren't satisfied: they believed that Remco, despite his incredible performance on the treadmill test, had 'clocked off' too early. In their opinion, he hadn't hit the wall yet, that he needed to be even harder on himself – despite that 18 kilometres per hour, despite his tender age, still only 17 years old. 'We spoke to Remco about that,' says Fred. And we gave him an unequivocal message: if you can't sweat it out, then you can't win. Remco took this message on board immediately, he decided he would get past that wall.'

Fred Vandervennet: 'That treadmill test, that was exceptional. Phew...' You know what happened with that treadmill test: it went into an email as an attachment. And Patrick Evenepoel sent that email to Kevin De Weert, the man behind the Belgian Cycling Federation's climb project. A few weeks passed between the moment the treadmill test was con-ducted and the email was sent to Kevin. During that interval, Fred re-ceived another phone call from the Evenepoel family.

But it wasn't Patrick who phoned this time. It was Remco.

Remco said: 'Fred, I'm giving up football. I'm going to cycle.'

Fred didn't answer immediately. 'I was quiet *for a moment*,' he says now. And then Fred said: 'What? What did you say?'

'I'm going to cycle, coach,' Remco repeated.

Fred gulped momentarily and couldn't help pointing out the dangers of cycling to Remco: there are a lot of falls, it's a sport that comes with many risks, and Remco must take that into account. And was he aware that there might not really be much money to be made in the races? In any case, not as much as in football, surely? There was some back-and-forth chitchat, and Fred tried to get him to talk it over with PSV – couldn't they convince him in the Netherlands to at least reconsider? But, re-counts Fred: 'No, his decision was firm. And once it gets into his head, you'll never get it out. Remco was going to cycle.'

About a week or two after the conversation between Remco and Fred, Patrick and Agna also discovered that their son was going to become a cyclist. The way they found out was through a rather mundane, every-day occurrence: Patrick had noticed that his own racing bike often dis-appeared from the garage – there was just one person who could have ridden it. It can't be true, Patrick had thought, but he'd kept quiet. Agna had also had a presentiment but it was of a different order. It was her mothering instinct at work again: something was up with Remco, Agna found him to be moody, her son didn't seem happy. Something wasn't right.
Remco was forced to admit: 'Phone Fred, he'll explain it all.'
From that day onwards, Remco was a rider in the making.
Patrick and Fred took on the challenge together – that was a condition set by Agna: 'If he's going to go all out training for it, then I want Remco to do it with Fred.' Schedules were drawn up in accordance with the 'Vandervennet principle': a cyclist must ride and learn to cover a dis-tance as quickly as possible. A first training session was scheduled im-mediately: Patrick, Fred, and Remco set off to the Ardennes. A 120-kilometre route was mapped out from Tilff – it was the regular course Fred had ridden with other riders who wanted to make it: Yannick Eijssen, for example. Or Jürgen Roelandts. And Tom Boonen.
This is what Remco had to say after 120 kilometres in the hills around Liège:

'Fred, I'm worn out. I'm completely *knackered!*'

Fred thought that was normal.

Because he said: 'Do you know how fast you rode, Remco? You registered an average of 32 kilometres per hour! On your dad's bike!' Fred knew that this was exceptionally good. He knew that from his notes, where he'd recorded that other youngsters had completed that course at an average speed of 28 kilometres per hour. That's when Fred and Patrick knew that Remco would be able to climb. And then there was Kevin and the Federation's climb project still to come...

7

'KEEPING PEOPLE'S DREAMS ALIVE.'

When Fred Vandervennet had got into his car to follow Remco in his very first race – the 2017 Vlaams-Brabant provincial championship for juniors, a time trial – he saw that things were going wrong immediately after the start: Remco took the first right-hand bend and veered into the grass verge, struggling to stay upright. There was Remco, in his neutral jersey, riding his father's bike. 'Or had Patrick Verschueren fitted *handle-bars* to it? I don't know, I can't remember.' In any case: Remco wasn't able to steer. He couldn't estimate his speed in a bend. In the beginning, yes, that was a problem. But Remco was fearless, that helped. Remco was now completely hooked on cycling and – we have to be honest – paying less attention to school. Fred sensed that and it concerned him. At school in Schepdaal, where Remco had ended up after his adventures in Anderlecht and Eindhoven, he encountered a headmistress who gave Remco a lot of freedom to pursue his ambition and dream of becoming a cyclist – 'An exceptional woman,' says Fred. Remco started travelling abroad more often then and he switched to distance learning. But it wasn't a simple matter, nor was it easy. 'Especially since his mother, Agna, valued school so much,' says Fred. 'I tried to help in whatever way I could. The only thing was: I could definitely teach Remco how to race, but I couldn't teach him how to study. I've never told Agna that. But Remco rapidly became so good at racing that Agna realised her son had huge potential. She acquiesced to Remco dedicating himself to racing.' Fred continued to train Remco, switching to a regimen of two sessions a day: in the morning with a time trial bike and in the afternoon with a regular road bike. 'Time and again, we pushed a little harder,' says Fred, picking up a sheet of paper and a pencil again. 'I made a schedule with symbols for him. Shall I draw it for you? You'll recognise it straight away.' Fred draws a straight line to represent flat kilometres. Then a wave shape, for the kilometres up – indeed – a rolling course, in the Flemish Ardennes, for example. Third diagram: peaks and valleys, for mountain training in Spain. Next? A flat line with a sprinkling of blocks: a block is a period of intense training – 'I was the first one to do this,' says Fred. Fifth? Hill training! Sixth: a line to indicate short interval training – three sets of 15 times 200 metres, for example. The seventh – and final – line with symbols: a mixture of all of the preceding, a bit of flat, uphill, solid climb work, fast successive blocks; in short, mixed training. Remco kept to that schedule, worked on it for weeks and showed his character. He got better and better.

At this point, Vandervennet wants to get a bit personal. By now, Remco had achieved a lot and was undoubtedly on his way as a young cyclist. We were now into 2018, and from 30 March to 2 April of that year, the Ster van Zuid-Limburg took place. The first stage was a short time trial of 5 kilometres from Mopertingen to Mopertingen, which was won by Joe Laverick from the United Kingdom. Remco was second in the same time as the winner – 7'30" (it came down to tenths of a second). The Dane, Mattias Skjelmose, won the second stage, with Remco finishing eighteenth some 6 seconds behind, in a large chasing group.

The third stage featured that moment that sends a shiver down Fred's spine.

'I followed that stage,' he says. 'Riders were falling, Remco jumped onto the pavement and crashed into a house. Hit so hard, the people from the Red Cross thought he was dead.'

Fred's perception is that Remco remained unconscious for a very long time, up to a full 10 minutes. In all probability, the timeframe isn't accurate, but it's the feeling that counts here: how a young rider crashed before the eyes of his followers and was now motionless. Then the surprise continuation of Fred Vandervennet's story: after that long period of uncertainty, Remco got back on his bike. 'And went on to finish this stage.' Did that really happen? Indeed, it did. The results you can find online for the third stage of the Ster van Zuid-Limburg – held on 1 April 2018 over a distance of 126.6 kilometres between Landen and Landen – back up Fred's account. A group of 35 riders took part in the victory sprint after 3 hours, 7 minutes, and 48 seconds. The Brit Alfie George took first place ahead of Tuur Dens. Remco finished in 67th position in a time of 9 minutes and 25 seconds.

That evening, Fred got a phone call from Remco. He recounted the fall and what he felt: pain, of course, and uncertainty – what ought he to do now? 'I told him in no uncertain terms to get back on his bike again the next day. I believed this was the best way to avoid becoming scared. Initially, Remco was against this approach, I felt resistance. But in the end he conceded. Remco would take part in the final stage.'

On 2 April, Fred Vandervennet was again present. Accompanied by his grandson Yari, he followed the race from Buvingen to Borlo – a distance of 118.5 kilometres. Yari, a young lad of 16 and the apple of his grandfather's eye, was with him for the first time. 'When he was born, Yari experienced a certain amount of oxygen deprivation,' says Fred. 'That's why his motor skills are not what they should be.' Yari immediately took to Remco, the young man of roughly his own age who often hung out with his grandpa. And on this day, 2 April 2018, he would witness Remco riding in a real race. 'But what can you say to your grandson?' says Fred. 'That there's a good chance Remco won't be able to keep up? That you don't know whether he'll win? Because Remco was black and blue all over, on account of his fall the previous day. Would Remco actually be able to finish the Ster van Zuid-Limburg?' For that reason, Fred decided to find a place with Yari where they could see the riders pass by twice – once going uphill and once coming downhill. What Remco demonstrated that day was – as Fred himself says – 'abnormal'. Remco rode away from all and sundry, winning with a lead of 1'28" over a group of nine pursuers.

On that day, Yari became Remco's biggest supporter. He travelled by bus to the World and European Championships. Fred saw (and continues to see) this happen with a mixture of joy and pride – Yari has become a well-received figure in Remco's world. Yari has become 'the champion's four-leaved clover'. On meeting one another, Remco and Yari embrace – could this be the making of a lifelong friendship? Most probably.

Fred continued to coach and train Remco until Remco turned professional. Then he had to part company with him. It was a painful message for Patrick and Agna to convey – but that's the way it was now. 'In a professional team, they work with different values and different methodologies. I'm aware of that,' says Fred. 'I don't work with training peaks nor do I work with data entered into a computer. I work with my tongue, with my words, with my insights. A computer gets in the way of creative thinking.'

Fred, Agna, Patrick: their bond remains in place and goes on. They watched together as Remco powered his way to the pinnacle of cycling. Messages back and forth between them feel really good, just before the start of the first Tour de France, for example. The three of them think back to the early days and give each other a virtual, digital hug. And from the bubble of the Tour, Remco sends thumbs-ups to Fred. Will Remco win his first Tour de France? 'Who knows,' says Fred – 'the riders have only been on the road for a week, a lot can happen, so much can go well, so much can go wrong, and before long it will be the mountains, the highest mountains.' What does he think will happen in Nice?

Fred ponders for a moment and then says: 'Do you know what's so great? That Remco gives people something to dream about. Is it possible that a Belgian might win the Tour again, almost fifty years after Lucien Van Impe? Whether it happens this year or next year, or maybe never, in itself that's not so important. What does count: Remco is keeping people's dreams alive. Go for it, Remco! Make sure the people keep dreaming!'

No one knew then, in the early days of July 2024, that Remco would bring his fellow countrymen to ecstasy, no one suspected then that he would cycle his way towards the podium of the Tour de France.

No one knew then that at the end of that same month of July, Remco would forever take his place in the world of the very greatest athletes – and he was still only 24 years young.

No one knew then that on 3 August 2024, Remco would be celebrated worldwide in the newspapers, after all the dreams that had now been realised: 'He had become double Olympic champion at the same Games, a unique achievement in history. From his victory in the time trial to a photo to be framed: alone, under the Eiffel Tower, holding up the bike. 'Iconic,' declares *AS*, the Spanish sporting newspaper: '*Ya era doblemente campeón olímpico en unos mismos Juegos, algo único en la historia. De su victoria en la prueba contrarreloj a una foto para enmarcar: solo, debajo de la Torre Eiffel y levantando la bici. Icónico.'*

And this is what *L'Équipe* wrote: 'Evenepoel has pulled off an unbelievable double. A week after the time trial, the Belgian triumphed in the road race after an almost 40-kilometre raid through the streets of Paris. He took his time to celebrate, with the Eiffel Tower in the background. He was far too strong for the 89 other riders. Once again, "The Little Cannibal" showed his insatiable appetite. He has written history.' How lyrical does it sound in French? And what about *La Gazetta dello Sport* then? In Italian, the song of praise goes like this: '*Remco Evenepoel regala uno storico bis al Belgio, conquistando anche la medaglia d'oro nella prova su strada, dopo avere trionfato in quella a cronometro: nessuno nella storia dei Giochi aveva ottenuto un risultato così prestigioso nella stessa edizione.*' Or: 'A triumphant parade, an achievement for the history books.'

8

'I SAID TO THE
OTHER GUYS:
"DON'T WORRY!
SAY THAT I'VE
MADE UP MY MIND!
WE'RE TAKING
REMCO WITH US."
AND WE WON!'

Back to Remco's first race, the provincial championship of Vlaams-Brabant for juniors.

The Sunday of the time trial, Remco was tenth. Arne Marit won, ahead of Stan Van Tricht. Arne and Stan are now – as this book is being written in 2024 – fully fledged professional riders. Remco's shortfall on the winner: 43 seconds. 'That tenth place, it didn't both me that much,' says Patrick Verschueren. 'What mattered most to me was that Remco hadn't lost much time on the leaders. At that time, Thibaut Ponsaerts was a leading performer among the novices and juniors. He figured as a kind of benchmark for me at the time. In the time trial he was fourth, with Remco a mere 30 seconds behind him. That meant something, after all.'

Patrick Verschueren faced a dilemma after the time trial: his team was actually full, leaving no room for an additional cyclist. And yet... he didn't know exactly what it was, a kind of feeling or intuition; yeah, what was it? 'I sensed it. I recognised when such a kid had something in him, something more than the others. The same feeling I'd had with Olav Kooij, with Vito Braet, Harm Vanhoucke, Stan Van Tricht, Cédric Beullens.' Patrick Verschueren had also had that feeling with Frank van den Broek. Do you know him? Not half! The young puncher who in the 2024 Tour propelled his captain Romain Bardet to victory and the yellow jersey in the first stunning stage near Florence (Italy).

Patrick Verschueren also had that special feeling about Remco, just like Kevin De Weert and Fred Vandervennet had before him.

'I made him a proposal,' says Verschueren. 'I wanted to make a deal. If he finished his first real race next week, then I wanted to include Remco in my team. That was a race somewhere in Brabant, in Zemst I guess. I was there with a team composed of many West Flemish and Dutch riders. And Remco? Yes, he rode in that race as well. Just that, nothing more.' After the deal, Forte's team had to set to work with their newest acquisition. 'Because Remco could do nothing yet. We had to teach him all of that. But that was normal, the youngster had never raced before.'

And the fact he often fell, as Kevin De Weert already mentioned? Was that so? Patrick Verschueren nods: 'Fell? Yes, Remco fell. I'm going to tell you the story of that *first race* he was allowed to ride for me. That was the Tour de L'Eure in France. A nice course, a difficult one for juniors.' If you browse the organisation's website, you'll see a number of riders that the people of the Tour de l'Eure are proudly showcasing. Under the section entitled 'Pro après Le Tour de l'Eure Juniors', you can read the names of young riders who once participated in the Tour de l'Eure and have gone on to become professionals. Benoît Cosnefroy, Warren Barguil, Pascal Eenkhoorn, Lyndsay De Vylder, Mathieu Burgaudeau, Liam Slock, Alexis Gougeard, Kévin Vauquelin – indeed, the rider from Arkéa-B&B Hotels who won the second stage of the Tour in Bologna in 2024 so magnificently – and, of course, Remco Evenepoel.

'There was also a team time trial in Le Tour de l'Eure,' says Verschueren. The Forte juniors wanted to win it, but they had a problem – at least, they thought they did. 'Those lads came to me in advance,' says Patrick. 'They were panicking a bit. "Coach," they said, "we're going to lose that time trial because Remco can't ride with the *bike* yet." But I said to them: "Don't worry! Say that I've made up my mind. We're taking Remco with us." And we won!' Patrick Verschueren may have told his riders not to worry, but he himself was worried. Because, as he says: 'If you ride up a mountain, then you also have to ride down it. And Remco can't do that yet. He fell heavily in a descent! To put it bluntly: I'm always looking out for his wheel now. Remco had broken his nose, he needed to go to the hospital. I called mother Agna and father Patrick, and I told them that "we had a little problem with the kid" – I referred to Remco as *the kid* – and then Patrick said he was coming to France, that he'd jump in his car immediately. I told Remco that his dad was on his way but Remco said that wasn't necessary. Because he wanted to follow the race next to me in the car the following day, broken nose and all. 'Yes, but,' I said to Remco, 'that's not going to work, you're in no state after a fall like you had. I thought to myself: come on kid! Kid! His dad phoned me the Monday after: "Patrick," he said, "do you want to know something? Remco wants to start training." 'No,' says Patrick Verschueren. 'That wasn't normal.'

Fred Vandervennet still recalls that incident with the broken nose. But he asks himself: was the nose really broken? 'I don't actually know,' he says. 'What I do know is that Remco wanted to get past someone on a downhill bend. You don't do that, it's a mistake. In any case: his nose wasn't looking good. I think it was split. It didn't look nice, that's for sure. If you look closely at photos of Remco, you can still see the scars on his face.'

In the seventh race that Remco rode, on 1 July 2017, in Bollebeek, near Asse, Brussegem, Mazenzele, and Merchtem, he was the winner. Remco rode – certainly in Patrick Verschueren's perception – in front of the peloton the whole day. Great, of course, that first victory, that beaming lad in his black jersey with yellow accents from Forte. But by then, it was high time to take the next steps. Remco was allowed to start in the more challenging junior races. Patrick: 'In his first races, he always rode in front of the peloton. If I were to take him to those bigger races with better riders, he would have to learn to ride in the peloton, he couldn't just ride away from those guys, I thought.' Remco was paying his dues – and that was a good thing. He learned how to behave in a breakaway, what to do if he had a puncture – 'I taught him to ride behind a car to get back in his group. Be careful! I taught him not to hang onto the car. Never! Never! I taught him that after getting a flat tyre, he had to hold back a bit, to tuck into the wheel of the dropped riders ahead of him. He picked all of that up. In that race where he got a flat tyre, he managed to get back to the leaders. He went for broke in the last round, on the cobblestones, as I'd instructed him to do, and we'd see afterwards how well it worked. In the end, he did get caught, and ultimately there were six men at the front sprinting for victory. Remco was sixth. I congratulated him then. You rode well.'

'Now I wanted to see what he could do in the mountains, the real mountains.' I took him to the Tour of the Basque Country. We wanted to win that tour, no messing, for serious. We didn't go just for the fun of it. I instructed Remco to get involved in the intermediate sprints. I knew that the Spaniards didn't put a lot of effort into it; they sprinted once and then that was it. We at Forte would approach it differently. After each intermediate sprint, we would race all out, we were going to attack.'

Remco understood that completely: he controlled the race and became the leader in the intermediate sprints classification. Then something strange happened – or better expressed: then something happened that was a sign of the strong will, the character of the great rider that the lad would become before long. It all happened on the podium of the *cérémonie protocollaire*, as it's beautifully named in the rich language of cycling life. 'Remco came up to collect his blue leader's jersey. Believe it or not, he'd put on different socks! Not socks from our team, nor socks displaying Forte's yellow and black colours. 'He started to give me an explanation there,' says Patrick Verschueren. 'About socks that were too warm. Socks this and socks that. About socks that didn't go with that blue jersey and so on and so on, driving me mad with his explanation. Of course, that wasn't on. Either we rode with yellow and black socks or we didn't ride. After some ado, he finally got the message.'
Patrick Verschueren apologises for the words he is about to say. But he has no choice but express it like this, he says: '*That little monkey!* Trying that on!' In other words, Remco dared to challenge.

In the Tour of the Basque Country for juniors, with the beautiful name 'Bizkaiko Itzukia', Evenepoel ultimately finished in second place. Ben Healy – now an outstanding professional – won the tour, and Oier Lazkano – already the Spanish champion among elite riders in 2023 – came third. In short, there was a quality field in the Basque Country. The final stage was a steep uphill section. Remco broke away with the winner from the previous year, I believe. On the final climb, Remco blasted away, for sure! I'd seen enough. I took note of it.'
Remco's riding style was remarkable. But there was more: 'We arrived there in the Basque Country a day before the race. That's how it went at the time. The organisers were honoured that riders from Belgium, France, and Italy were coming to race with them. They wanted to give us a warm welcome. You couldn't expect too much from it: we got a place

to sleep in a little school, and in the evening there was a reception with fries; all very simple, but well-intentioned. Patrick, Remco's father, was there too. "Come and join us," I said, "You don't have to sit there alone, just move over." Patrick came and sat with the team, I can still visualise it now. Patrick looked at his son and said: "Just watch, Remco won't eat the fries," he said. "He won't touch them.'" Remco didn't have a single fry.

That's when Patrick Verschueren knew for certain: 'What a boy!'

In the Basque Country, the news about that young Belgian was a hot topic of conversation. Here and there, some conversations were already taking place that anything could happen. Patrick Verschueren bumped into Joxean Matxin Fernández – just call me 'Matxin'. The Spaniard – or rather, the Basque – with the bald head was known in the peloton as the man with a nose for new talent. 'Patrick,' said Matxin, 'if you ever have another promising young rider, you must let me know.' Verschueren didn't hesitate for a moment: 'Write this down,' he said to the scout. 'I'm going to give you a name right now, do you have something to write with? It's not often that I'm wrong,' said Patrick.
'I said to Matxin: "Remco Evenepoel."'

Officially, Matxin is actually José Antonio Fernández Rodriguez. But in the cycling world, he is better known as Joxean Fernández Matxin, or Matxin for short. He was born in Basauri, in the Basque area of Spain. As of 2024, he is a manager at Team UAE, but in 2017 that was not yet the case. Back then he was the man who scouted for Patrick Lefevere's teams, in search of youngsters who might have what it takes to succeed in the world of elite cycling, a talent scout who went around the world, from competition to competition. In other words, he was the man who got in conversation with Patrick Verschueren.

'Hi, how are you,' said Joxean Fernandez Matxin on Sunday afternoon, 20 October 2024. 'I'm in Dubai,' he added. 'Tomorrow, I'm flying back home.'

This book's author sipped his coffee – black, no sugar – and listened to the story of the amiable Basque. It went like this, originally in a mixture of Spanish and English: 'Yes, it was in Basque Country, it was there indeed that I saw Remco competing for the first time. The history is that I was working with Patrick Lefevere as a scout. I still remember him as a youngster who rode with the juniors for Forte and was competing in the Tour of the Basque Country for the youth category. In the first stage that boy – this guy – was in the lead, in the first position, and he pushed on – pull, pull, pull. He took all the other riders along in his slipstream. But at every corner, things went wrong; he just couldn't take the bends properly – all day a lot of mistakes.' After that first stage, though, Matxin had seen enough: he didn't go and talk to the day's winner. I didn't go to the good riders, Ben Healy and Oier Lazkano.' He was really intrigued by the rider who missed the corners. 'I went up to Remco and told him that he was a superb rider. But I asked him how he could be getting it wrong so often – so many mistakes.'

Then Remco answered: 'But I'm a football player.'
And, he said: 'This is only my third race.'
Just a minute, says Matxin: 'Third or fourth race? I can't remember exactly any more. Had he just said that this was only his third or fourth race? In any case, he did say that he had ridden one or two races in Belgium. But that was about it.' Being from the Basque Country himself, Matxin knew what was to come on the second day of the Tour: an arduous stage with a tough climb. 'I told Remco that he should follow the advice I wanted to give him for that stage to the letter. According to me, he must stay at the back of the peloton to start with. Once the climb began, he could then move up to the front. Those were the instructions I fed him. Don't keep fighting the position before, hold back. And stay calm.'
Right: so the next day came that second stage. Matxin decided to follow Remco on the car – 'not in a car.' He still recalls what happened: 'Remco followed my instructions exactly. He continued to ride at the back of the peloton, and just when he was supposed to appear at the front, that's

exactly what he did too. He went full gas and he won the stage. I still remember it as though it were yesterday. In the end, Remco finished second in the overall classification of the 2017 edition of the Tour of the Basque Country for juniors.'

After the podium ceremony for that second stage, Matxin had to speak to Patrick Lefevere: 'I'm here with a Belgian rider, a golden guy!' After which, he went on to add: 'Believe me, this is a rider who we must have for the next five years.' Matxin thought it wasn't a bad idea to allow Remco to grow for two years first in Axel Merckx's strong development team. Whoever got included in that team could, in principle, prepare for a great career. 'Jasper Philipsen, Jonathan Narvaez, Mikkel Bjerg are examples,' says Matxin. 'After those two years, Remco should then progress to Patrick Lefevere's elite team.' That the approach was planned in this way will become apparent later on in this book, when other key figures talk about Remco's first months.

Patrick Lefevere listened attentively to the praise sung by his Spanish-Basque scout. Yet he did have some misgivings: the youngster that Matxin was talking about was still only a junior, and not only that, he was a former footballer. Did it really make sense to sign that young man for such a long time? Matxin still remembers that he was absolutely convinced of the talent he'd seen in the Basque Country – 'a super talent, believe me.' Not only had he said to Patrick Lefevere that Remco was a good cyclist, but he'd described him as 'a super champion.' 'It was the first time in my life that I'd said such a thing,' he recounts. 'Two months earlier, he was a football player. And now, he was already on this level.' Anyway, the conversation with Axel happened, and meanwhile, Matxin had moved to Team UAE, after consulting with Patrick Lefevere, and on good terms – 'there were no hard feelings.' Remco started his second year as a junior in 2018, about which there's more for you to read later. As you'll discover, Remco became a multiple winner. 'One day, there I was on the Tour,' Matxin goes on to say. 'There was a knock at the door of the UAE team bus. Patrick Lefevere was standing there, accompanied by Remco and his father. The inevitable had happened: Remco was included in Patrick Lefevere's team. Rather than going first to Axel Merckx, he'd immediately become a professional cyclist. Their visit spoke volumes about their gratitude, they really appreciated how much I'd believed in Remco. That's why I like the father, the mother, and Remco. They show such gratitude.' Remco showed that gratitude towards Matxin once again before the start of the final stage of the Tour of Spain in 2022 – the Vuelta that Remco would win. 'It was in Madrid,' says Matxin. 'He wanted to thank me, again.'

What makes Remco so strong? Matxin: 'I don't know. He's such a different rider. He's such a different champion. He is so different from all the riders I've got to know. Pure quality, a diamond, that's Remco. And because he had so little experience – after all, he was a footballer – he can only improve. Look, that's the difference with Tadej. Tadej is the perfect cyclist, he mastered the technique of cycling as a child, he's smart, and he also has the experience. Could Remco end up winning the Tour? In my opinion? Remco is a natural rider for the Tour. The mountains in the Tour de France are tailor-made for him: they're long, and you need to be able to sustain efforts of more than 20 minutes. These mountains demand power, power, power. And Remco has that power. It's different in the Giro. There you need to be more explosive, with shorter, powerful 5-minute efforts. That's less suited to Remco.'

And Matxin makes up his mind: 'Yes, Remco is a candidate for the Tour. Together with Tadej.'

Then the winter of 2017 arrived.
And ended the story of Remco with Patrick Verschueren and his team Forte.

9

'A FRIENDLY GUY,
VERY APPRECIATIVE.
THAT WAS A LAD
WHO KNEW WHAT
HE WANTED.'

Jef Robert is the chairman – and benefactor, sponsor – of the Royal Balense Cycling Club. Paul Laenen is the team captain there. The club has been in existence now for 75 years and is actually a non-profit organization. You know the team better under its commercial name: Acrog-Tormans. For some time now, it has also been linked to Quick Step, which features in small print on the riders' gear. Robert and Laenen's club is renowned for its excellent youth development programme. A number of riders who once did their training there became outstanding professionals: Jordi Meeus, Jonas Rickaert, Gerben Thijssen, Jenthe Biermans are just a few of them. Along with: Florian Vermeersch and Cian Uijtdebroeks – top-class riders, no less. Sometimes a young lad of around 14 would stay under the radar, simply because he was still developing physically and at a slightly slower rate than his peers – Kevin De Weert has also talked about this phenomenon. That wasn't a bad thing necessarily, as sometimes such a young rider would still progress significantly and might go on to win Milan-San Remo, many stages, and the green jersey in the Tour de France – we're talking about Jasper Philipsen of course. The lads can stay with Acrog-Tormans until they are eighteen, until the end of their time as juniors. Then they're ready for the next step-up: 'We produce good riders who can move on to the university of cycling. They find their place, for example, in the development teams of major elite squads,' says Jef Robert. But every now and then, a rider skips that category of development. Or no, we ought to express it differently: all of a sudden, there was a young man who was so exceptional that he unexpectedly made the leap from juniors to professionals. Suddenly, there he was, Remco Evenepoel.
Jef Robert and Patrick Laenen say in unison: 'Remco was exceptional.'

The fact that Remco ended up with Robert and Laenen's team was partly down to Patrick Verschueren's indiscretion. In all his enthusiasm, Patrick couldn't keep quiet about the impressive achievements of the young man from Schepdaal who had only just stopped playing football. When they were at a race somewhere in France, Laenen and Verschueren started to chat to each other. They immediately talked about that unbelievable chap who, in his first race – a time trial, no less – didn't lag much behind the youngsters who had been at it for a good deal longer. Of course, Patrick Verschueren wasn't the only one talking about Remco so enthusiastically. 'Everyone was keeping an eye on him,' say Robert and Laenen. 'Everyone wanted to work with him. Including us, at Acrog-Tormans.' The fact that Patrick had raced alongside father Evenepoel helped – they knew each other. But most of all, its strong reputation as a development team played a role in Remco's transfer. 'One day we got a call from Fred Vandervennet. As to whether we could talk about the youngster he was giving training to,' recounts Jef Robert.

A meeting? Robert agreed to this. He stands up and pours some coffee. 'Look, there, on that chair, that's where Fred sat. And Remco over there,' he continues. 'Remco was immediately enamoured with the programme that we rode with our team. He was attracted to the fact that we were welcome everywhere, we were invited all over Belgium and throughout Europe. And Remco knew that.'

'I immediately had a good feeling about Remco,' recounts Patrick Laenen. Laenen describes Remco in these words: 'A friendly guy, very appreciative. That was a lad who knew what he wanted.' And, he goes on to add: 'It just clicked. We had the ideal programme for him, we rode all the top events, with the best riders.'

Remco began training with us in the winter of 2018. He did well.
And he got a roommate: Stef Loos.
Patrick Laenen and Jef Robert must recount here the drama that took place on 17 March 2019 – Patrick Evenepoel has already mentioned it earlier in this book. It's the story of the awful outcome of the race in Hainaut and the loss of a friend. A young man was snatched from this life while doing what he loved: racing. The team, the coaches, the riders, and the parents had to say goodbye to their loved one.
'I asked Remco if he would like to say something at the funeral,' says Robert.
'Remco did want to,' says Robert.

'We stood there, in the small square in front of the church in Dessel. We had gathered there, all wearing a smart jersey,' say Laenen and Robert. 'A large crowd was present.'

Yes, Remco wanted to say something – what else can a young man do when his friend and companion, is no more? 'Remco had no notes with him and it looked as though he hadn't done any preparation. But there he stood, at the front of the church, facing all those people and all that sorrow. Remco spoke in the sweetest words you could imagine. Scarcely 19 years old, there he stood, a fullgrown man.'

Remco learned fast in his new team.

'We rode a time trial, somewhere in Limburg,' says Patrick Laenen. 'Remco caught up with the rider who'd left before him. But on the bends, that rider kept overtaking Remco. In each bend, Remco lost one or two, or even three seconds. I pointed this out to him. I told him that he needed to put in practice on his bend work. We did another time trial a couple of weeks later. What's going on, I thought when I saw what Remco was up to. I had to shut my eyes. The risks he was taking! He'd gone from one extreme to the other in just a few weeks: from a boy who was still afraid in the bends to a daredevil.' Laenen and Robert wonder how that is even possible. In actual fact it's quite simple: Remco is the embodiment of focus and drive. Robert puts it like this: 'Remco comes home and asks everyone with any knowledge – in this specific case – how you should take bends. He processes all this information in his head and then does something with it. What do you think has made him so good at descents?' Patrick Verschueren had also mentioned that: 'Give Remco a task and he throws himself into it completely. After his fall in that descent in the Tour de l'Eure, he spent hours watching videos he found on YouTube. Those recordings of heroic descents from major races showed him how he had to tackle it.'

The men from Acrog-Tormans had a habit of organising a test time trial during their spring training camp, always on the same course – 'with a 7-kilometre climb'. Remco was allowed to participate in 2018 – 'with a strong class', emphasizes Patrick Laenen. 'Each and every one of those guys wanted to prove himself, all of them wanted to show how strong they were. Macho behaviour.' On the day of the test time trial in 2018, something strange happened: after the new boy crossed the finish line, Patrick Laenen kept quiet about the time Remco had ridden. First, he needed a moment to recover from what the stopwatch was saying. 'I'd never seen a time like that before. Surely it couldn't be? But it was completely accurate: Remco's time was phenomenal.'

The only word with which Patrick Laenen is able to sum it up is: *'Wow.'*

Remco was getting better and better; he was growing and his bike skills were getting more refined. In short, Remco was an outstanding cyclist. He got more freedom in devising his programme. Although in fact this freedom wasn't completely needed. 'Remco wanted to do everything, anyway,' says Jef Robert. And, Patrick Laenen adds: 'He also won everything. Or almost everything.'

Remco was so incredibly good, his own teammates could no longer keep up with him. 'Sometimes we let them ride after him when he was once again leading on his own. "Try to follow him", we'd say. If they caught up with him, they would automatically end up with a good ranking.' At times, this led to frustration: at the Belgian championship team time trial, Remco had to hold back; after all, he had to arrive with at least three riders – that's just how a team time trial works. If he'd kept on pushing hard, he would have worn his teammates into the ground. The result? They weren't Belgian champions. Honestly? If Remco had ridden the team time trial on his own, he would have been Belgian champion in the team time trial individually.

Remco wore out his teammates; that's how strong he'd become. Isn't it remarkable: not so long ago in this story, the Forte riders were panicking because that new guy was to be included in a team time trial, and they'd protested: 'But coach! We'll lose! Remco, who can't ride with the *bike* yet.'

10

'REMCO, YOU MUST STAY SITTING IN THE PELOTON! YOU ARE NOT GOING TO RIDE IN FRONT. IS THAT UNDERSTOOD? IT'S AN ORDER, REMCO!'

Aubel-Thimister-Stavelot is a great course for juniors. It has everything: a team time trial, a steep climb, a descent, a peloton with brilliant riders. A formidable list of riders have won it over the years, including: Mikkel Bjerg, David Gaudu, Wilco Kelderman, Frank Vandenbroucke. And in second or third place: Lennert Van Eetvelt, Bjorg Lambrecht, Mads Pedersen, Guillaume Martin.

In 1962, it was won by a promising young man from Brussels: Eddy Merckx.

Because there were other races where they needed to have a delegation present, Acrog-Tormans lined up at the 2018 start with slightly fewer strong riders than planned. Patrick Laenen had brought his team leader along though: Remco Evenepoel. By now he had become European champion, and his name and fame were soaring, television broadcasters were gradually wanting to know more about that phenomenon – the kid from Brussels. 'RTBF, the French-speaking public broadcaster, came to make a report,' says Jef Robert. 'On the second day, before the start of the team time trial, they wanted to have a conversation with the team mates. And they wanted to film during the warm-up. The youngsters were a bit uneasy. "We'll have to try and keep up with Remco", they said.'

Jef Robert sympathised with Remco's fellow team members.

'Can you do it, guys?' I asked.

'No!' they said. 'We won't be able to keep up.'

'Look, they don't have to take the lead, you know!' says Jef.

'They just have to stay tucked in to Remco's wheel.'

'Or try to follow.'

Remco held himself back and encouraged his teammates: 'Come on, guys! Come on!'

They finished second, which was disappointing – for Remco.

Remco had also been disappointed the previous day, in the first stage on Friday. As per usual, he'd broken away, and there was only one person still with him. That youngster didn't take the lead; he was exhausted. All he could do was follow, suffer, and die on Remco's wheel. But he managed to stay on the wheel right up to the finish until it was time for the sprint. The youngster on Remco's wheel could sprint, that was a known fact among the junior peloton.

'Look,' says Jef Robert. He gets his mobile phone out and searches for a photo. 'Here you see the moment when Remco realised he'd been beaten. Notice how he threw his arm in the air, out of frustration, out of rage? That youngster who wins here had not been in front for a single metre. Not one metre. Not because he didn't want to be. Simply because he couldn't.'

Who was that winning youngster? Biniam Girmay.

There sat Remco with all his pent-up anger, frustrated after two stages and no victory. 'He won the third stage,' says Robert. 'With a 15-minute lead, or thereabouts. In any case, he again rode the entire time in the lead, all on his own.' And according to Patrick Laenen, that was a problem: 'He was always away and so he wasn't learning how to ride in a peloton. In the long-term, that was a disadvantage.' In response, Acrog-Tormans had an idea: they sent Remco to the race in Wuustwezel. 'A race on a flat course, ten times out of ten it ends in a mass sprint. No one gets away from the peloton there. Remco did want to break away again, for sure. But we'd forbidden him to do that. We forced him to stay put, to get the feel for riding in a group, surrounded by his teammates. Only at 15 kilometres from the finish was he allowed to go hell for leather, only then could he go *full gas*. And away he went,' says Robert. 'As I said, ten times out of ten there would be a mass sprint in Wuustwezel. With the exception of this one time, though.'

Remco became Flemish champion in the time trial for juniors, and he became Flemish champion on the road.
Remco became Belgian champion in the time trial for juniors, and he became Belgian champion on the road.
Remco became European champion in the time trial for juniors, and he became European champion on the road.
Remco became world champion in the time trial for juniors, and he became world champion on the road.

All of that in 2018.

Or, in the words of Robert and Laenen: 'He simply won everything.'
Laenen and Robert were convinced that despite his dominance and despite all his victories, that Remco had not yet reached his peak. They knew that he would keep on growing: 'Purely and simply because he still hadn't trained that much, nor had he been racing for long. He knew how to train – football had taught him that – and he was receiving excellent guidance from Fred Vandervennet. In short: he still had huge potential for growth.'

Plus, the fact that: 'Remco's character was one of cast-iron determination coupled with enormous drive. Added to which, he didn't show the slightest fear of failure. If he received criticism, then it was a signal for him to step up another notch, nothing more. Remco rode with his legs. And with his head.' Jef Robert makes a bold comparison – as he describes it himself. 'What Remco does and thinks is reminiscent of what Muhammad Ali, the greatest boxer ever, did: Ali decided for himself how and when he would attack, he determined for himself how the flow of his actions should come together.'

Anyone looking for quotes from Ali, will come across this one: 'Champions aren't made in gyms. Champions are made from something they have deep inside them – a desire, a dream, a vision. They have to have the skill, and the will. But the will must be stronger than the skill.' Doesn't this apply to Remco too? 'Champions aren't made in gyms. Champions are made from something they have deep inside them – a desire, a dream, a vision.' Isn't that right?

In the words of Jef Roberts, Remco graduated from the school of juniors at the age of eighteen. He was ready to step up to a major development team, within a large professional elite squad. It would have been the step that every rider of that age takes. But, as you know, that step didn't happen. Remco immediately became a professional cyclist in Patrick Lefevre's Quick Step team. Choosing not to move up to the under-23s was the best choice Remco could ever make. There was nothing more for Remco to learn there,' says Jef Robert.

The people at Acrog-Tormans had prepared the young junior for a life among the real men. They look back on that now with pride.
Patrick Laenen: 'Remco is a great champion. A likeable, grateful guy. A chap who goes to get beers for the mechanics and soigneurs after a tough race. That says a lot, doesn't it?'
Jef Robert: 'A young man with character, with a lot of balls.'
And furthermore, they say: 'He's still going to grow.'
We're having a fresh coffee together, and it tastes great.
'Remco is going to win a lot more yet,' is Laenen and Robert's conclusion. He's ready for more, much more.'

The next day, Remco became the Olympic champion in the time trial. A week later, he became the Olympic champion in the road race in an overwhelming manner. You'll find that story later in this book.

11

'REALLY! THAT
CAR TOOK MY
WHEEL WITH
IT! I'M NOT
KIDDING!'

In 1981, Carlo Bomans became Belgian junior champion on the road. Eight years later, in 1989, he did the same again in the professionals. Then he surprised everyone by beating Eddy Planckaert in Waregem in the sprint for the tricolour jersey. It became Carlo's greatest victory – he also won Dwars door België, the E3 Prize, and stages in weeklong tours like Paris-Nice, the Tour of Belgium, the Tour of the Mediterranean, and the Ster van Bessèges. And he won the team time trial in the 1993 Tour, alongside Mario Cipollini, Franco Ballerini, Johan Museeuw, and Wilfried Peeters. His team? GB-MG Maglificio, a kind of distant forerunner of what later (in various forms) became the Wolfpack. In short: Carlo Bomans clocked up an impressive list of achievements in cycling. After 1998, he drew a line under his professional career, forced to do so by serious injuries.

'I wasn't someone who fell often. But if I did fall, so to speak, something always got broken,' Carlo recounts quite expressively. And he gives an example: in the Tour of Luxembourg, there was a piece of metal on the road, Bomans was riding in second position in the peloton, and he hadn't seen that piece of metal.

'All I can remember now is crack, crack, and that piece of metal flying into my front wheel. Everything was broken, everything gone, we weren't wearing helmets back then, so, there you go. The vertebrae in my neck were affected and my face had to be patched up again.' Or again: in the Ster van Bessèges, he broke his hip... In short, it was no laughing matter.

But not the end of the world: Carlo continued on his way in the world of cycling, succeeding José De Cauwer in 2005 as the national coach for the professional riders, got a world champion with Philippe Gilbert in 2012, and in 2016 became the national coach for juniors.

Yes, says Carlo: 'That story about Kevin De Weert and the email from Evenepoel's father is completely true.' They were scouting together for the European Championship, which in 2017 was to be held in Herning (Denmark) at the end of the summer. And then it arrived, that mail, it really did. Too late though, it's true. Together with the results of a performance test, that's also true. 'But I noticed that those results were from a treadmill test,' says Carlo. 'In actual fact, there wasn't much we could do with them. But Erwin Koninckx, our experienced exercise physiologist, could see behind those results and concluded that they were serious numbers.' The rest, as they say, is history: the people from Belgian Cycling made an exception for the young footballer from Schepdaal, he was allowed to join them in the Ardennes, didn't do badly there. Carlo also noticed that Remco carried more kilos than the – let's call them thus – already proper cyclists. But, says Carlo: 'He wasn't fat by any means. He had muscle, or more precisely, the wrong muscle. He was still built like a footballer. But he lost those kilos in next to no time.' And that was noticeable: Remco always positioned himself at the back of the group during training, out of fear of making the other youngsters fall. Because he had never raced before. That was obvious from another fact: Remco rode his first race – the renowned time trial – 'on an ordinary bike,' says Carlo. 'The other guys all had time trial bikes.'

Carlo followed from a distance what was happening with that new boy. 'But I really encountered him for the first time in the time trial in memory of Igor Decraene, in Waregem.'

Igor was a promising time trial rider, who in 2013 became Belgian and world champion in the junior category. Igor would have made it as a cyclist. But a year later, on 30 August 2014, his luck ran out in Zulte. He stayed forever 18 years old. From then on, the memory of Igor as a cyclist would only be kept alive in a Memorial.

'I have to be honest,' says Carlo, 'in that time trial, Remco's technique on the bends was non-existent. Twice he went off the road. But that was to be expected. Remco hadn't been a novice, he hadn't been a newcomer. Remco had never been a cyclist at all. Remco was a retired footballer who still had to learn how to cycle, so to speak.' But: Remco was actually second, behind Loran Cassaert. If you look up the results for the 2017 Igor Decraene Memorial, you will notice something rather striking: of the 24 cyclists listed in the results, 23 were riding for a club – from Isorex to Meubelen Gaverzicht and Van Moer Logistics. One rider had registered as an individual on that 16th of July; that boy (still) had no team: Remco Evenepoel. That's when it all started happening for Remco.

Carlo continued to watch in amazement as the new boy's results got better and better. 'And then I decided to take him with me to the World Championship in Bergen, Norway. What Kevin De Weert has already said is no less than the truth: In just a few months, Remco had become so good that I simply had to take him with me. He had already achieved such fantastic results, really impressive.'

Carlo laughs. And goes on to say: 'Initially, Remco was disappointed. Why? Because he couldn't ride in the WC time trial. He felt it was unfair, after all hadn't he already shown how good he was in that discipline? But there were others who were better at the time – like Ilan Van Wilder, for example. I only allowed Remco to start in the road race.' That World Championship on the road was a disaster, as Carlo Bomans now describes it, seven years on: 'After 3 kilometres, Remco had already fallen.' Bomans had nevertheless taken precautions; he'd assigned someone to Remco who was supposed to position the team leader – that being Remco – at the front of the peloton as quickly as possible. But well, that didn't help. 'We were allowed to start that day with six riders, and five of them fell to the ground. Remco fell three times, and after the third fall, I told him he had to stop. He was cut to pieces all over, and he wasn't allowed to continue riding. How did he react to that? He was upset, to put it mildly. You know, Remco couldn't do much about those crashes actually. The cobblestones on the course were wet, riders got tangled up, and before he knew it, he'd joined them as well.'

That evening, after the failed World Championship, something strange happened. Carlo Bomans came in to the hotel where the team was staying and passed by the rooms. 'I heard Remco lost it,' says Carlo. 'Not towards the teammates sleeping next to him in his room, but in response to the reactions he read on Facebook and Twitter. People were negative about his performances, and there were also quite a few jealous comments from other juniors who hadn't been allowed to come and felt passed over. They were reactions in the manner of: "That Remco only just waltzed in and there he is already at the World Championship. And look what a good job he did," things like that. That affected Remco, it really got to him. But in any case, the season was over after that World Championship; we could wrap up the year.'

Carlo noticed that Remco had trained well over the winter: 'He looked sharp, and then we got started. He was now allowed to actually ride with the core of the national team. He was determined to ride Gent-Wevelgem. That wasn't a great success. In the run-up to the Kemmelberg, Remco was at the rear. He managed to move up once, but the next time it didn't work. The peloton broke away and he wasn't with it.'

And then: Remco came up with a brand new idea. He wanted to ride Paris-Roubaix.

Carlo says: 'I asked him: "Paris-Roubaix? Remco, really? Paris-Roubaix?" That's what he wanted.'

Then Remco said: 'Yes, that's what I want to do! And I'm not kidding.'

Carlo says: 'Do you know what, Remco? I'm going to take you.'

It was a dry edition, the 2018 one. The cobblestones weren't a problem. Remco was perfectly positioned, they were entering the final, and there was still everything to play for.

Then we got a message over the radio: Remco had a problem with his bike. He needed a bike change. That got done quickly.'

In the support vehicle, a conversation unfolded between Carlo and mechanic Dominique. It was about the bike change. Carlo wondered what was actually wrong with the bike, as there appeared to nothing at all wrong with it. Dominique saw that too – no flat tyre, no other fault. Yet Remco had indicated that his handlebars were broken. What was going on? The handlebars had become slightly out of alignment when Remco rode over a pothole. But that's all that was wrong. Still, Remco was in the zone, wanted to win, didn't want any equipment with a flaw, and continued riding on a reserve bike, one from the Belgian Cycling Federation. 'We arrived at Carrefour de l'Arbre. Remco was sitting between the vehicles. I found my place with my own support car at the front of the race.'

Carlo was keeping contact with the other people in the race.

Remco was on his way, they announced.

He was in the slipstream of the Dutch riders on his way to the front of the race.

'There he is,' they said.

'He's coming.'

But Remco didn't turn up.

Where was he?

Carlo: 'He had a puncture.'

And, he goes on to add, with a smile on his face: 'Remco's explanation afterwards was that no support vehicle had wanted to stop; only the neutral car had actually done so.' From here on out, it turns into a wild story about a wheel that disappeared, about the neutral mechanic from that neutral support vehicle who'd taken that wheel, about Remco now left behind with a bike that had only one wheel, about Carlo's astonishment, and about Remco's determination to stick to that version of events – 'Yes, that neutral van took my wheel!' But as Carlo says: the internet set the seal on the truth. 'Images appeared on various channels showing Remco walking on the last cobblestone section with his bike, with one wheel on it. Only: he was holding the other wheel in his hand. Later, he'd thrown it away, out of temper. That wheel will still be lying there somewhere. Or no, that's not true. It will have gone already. In any case, Remco was angry, incredibly angry. He then started walking through the fields until the broom wagon picked him up and brought him to Roubaix. In the meantime, he had time to come up with the story of the neutral van. Because after all, he'd thrown away a wheel that belonged to the Federation.

Carlo ponders briefly. And then says: 'Yes, Remco can lose it. If things didn't go his way, he could get angry. Really angry. And he didn't want people thinking that he wasn't up to it. He was still bothered by the idea that people would think that he, the new man in the race, still hadn't earned his seat.'

But, says Carlo: 'There was no longer any doubt. Remco was going to make it. As he went on to prove in the next race I took him to with the national selection. That was the Peace Race in the Czech Republic.'

'CAN I DROP HIM NOW, COACH? WAIT A BIT LONGER, REMCO! AND NOW, COACH, CAN I NOW? CAN I DROP HIM NOW? WAIT JUST A LITTLE BIT LONGER, REMCO. AND AWAY HE WENT.'

The Peace Race was known among the juniors as the Cours de la Paix, says Carlo Bomans. It was a tough course though not all that long, just four days, from Thursday to Sunday. In 2018, it took place from 3 to 6 May. Six years on, Carlo Bomans sums up Remco's performance: 'That's where it totally exploded.'

The first ride was a difficult stage, comparable to a course in the Ardennes. 'You have to race against the best riders from all those other countries there,' Bomans says. 'That was no small feat.' Carlo went for an appropriate tactic: he wanted his juniors – in that international chaos – not to be too far back in the peloton and to be able to move together over the inclines.

'They rode upwards,' says Carlo.
And then they made a loop: 'So, down the loop and then back up what they had just gone down.' Carlo repeats once more: it was best for them to keep together as much as possible up to the top of the first climb, not to lose too much time. Only: just before the top, Remco broke away, he was gone. He rode that entire loop alone at the front for no end of kilometres, until he was eventually reeled in at the end. 'They caught up with him, the pursuers, it was as much as he could do to just hang on, but he didn't win.' A time trial was scheduled for the next day – 'I think he won that,' says Carlo. 'Or did he come second? No, he won it, of course he did. And he was leader.' During the next stage, which took place in the afternoon, the Belgian team lost a rider in the form of Steven Pattyn.

'Steven was in a bad state, I had to be on standby at the hospital,' says Carlo.
'The riders in the competition were more or less left to themselves to decide how they would race. Look at the stage in the morning, discuss it among yourselves and see how you want to approach it,' says Carlo. The following day's stage was a tough one. What they agreed on was to not attack too early, wait, and then put everything into the final lap: 'Make sure no one takes off who could be a threat to Remco's leader's

jersey, that was the pack drill.' But Remco had other plans: he broke away in the very first lap and there was only one man who could keep up with him: Karel Vacek.

Remco rode in the lead with Vacek tucked in behind his wheel. Might it not be better to let him too do some work at the front as well, Carlo had suggested – he had returned to the race after a visit to the hospital where he made arrangements for Steven's repatriation. Perhaps they could strike a deal: take Vacek with him, so the two of them could gain more of a lead, and let him win – 'Ah, why not?' Remco agreed but Vacek was not strong enough. Or rather, we should say it the other way round: Remco was far too strong, as simple as that. Vacek dropped back.

What now? Carlo bangs his hand on the table as we drink our coffee. We take a moment to swallow it. 'Remco stopped. He waited until Vacek caught up with him again. And Vacek won the stage.' Carlo laughs and shakes his head. 'Yes, exactly, yes,' I say. 'If you can win, then that's what you should do, Remco. If he has to drop off, then you shouldn't wait, Remco.' But he thought otherwise – an agreement was an agreement. He had promised Vacek that he could win, so Vacek did win.'

The next day – in the final stage – Remco left everyone for dead.
'What is it with that boy?' the coaches of the other teams asked.
Hmm, was Carlo's reply. 'What is it?'
Remco won the Peace Race, the Course de la Paix, by a large margin. After less than a year in the peloton, he was now slowly but surely making a name for himself. Sporza – the sports channel of the public broadcaster VRT – rated Remco's performances strong enough for a first in-depth write-up. From today's perspective, in 2024, that write-up is nice to read again: it all had yet to really happen but the admiration for so much audacity was already bursting through the words. This is the complete piece, frank and straight from the heart:

The headline was: 'Remco Evenepoel is lord and master in the Peace Race: not Ben Merckx'

And then, in the introduction:

Remco Evenepoel is making a serious name for himself in the world of cycling. The 18-year-old junior, who stopped playing football at Anderlecht in 2016, won the Peace Race in the Czech Republic in an impressive manner. He won two stages and took all the jerseys. 'I'm not Merckx: he's him and I'm me.'

The body text went on to say:

'Evenepoel showed on Tuesday that he is in fine form: he won the junior time trial in the Belgian championship in Vresse-sur-Semois, posting a faster time than the winner among the under-23 riders. Straight after that, Evenepoel flew with the Belgian team to the Czech Republic, where he was hard at it from Thursday to Sunday in one of the most prestigious stage races for juniors. He made his mark there on all four days: in the first stage, he rode more than 60 km solo in the attack. That didn't succeed, but he sprinted with his pursuers to finish in fifth place. The first part of the second stage was a time trial over 11.5 kms. He won this one and got the leader's jersey. "I was overjoyed about that because it was the first yellow jersey of my life." Evenepoel, an Ardennes type who can time trial and climb, predicted even then that he might be able to keep the jersey "because I feel good on the ascents." And that's what happened. In the queen stage on Saturday, the talented Belgian had to concede only to the Czech Karel Vacek, while registering the same time. Yesterday, the crowning achievement followed. In the final stage to Terzin, he dropped all and sundry with an attack along the way: no matter what the others tried, they couldn't catch up again. Evenepoel won by a margin of 1 minute and 17 seconds. In the final standings, he had a lead of 1 minute and 55 seconds over the Dane Mattias Skjelmose Jensen and 3 minutes and 53 seconds over the Norwegian Ludwig Fischer Aasheim. The fanfare of praise rang loud and clear: "It's gratifying to hear them calling me the new Eddy Merckx, but that's much too strong a claim. I'm not like him: he was an extraordinary rider, and it's not right to compare me to him. He was him and I'm me. I'm just really happy with what I've achieved. But I also want to emphasize the strength of our team. The guys help me a great deal. I wouldn't have won without their fantastic support for me on the climbs. They deserve a huge thank you," remarks Evenepoel, modest to the end.'

After the Peace Race, Remco was allowed to go to Morbihan, in France. The first climb came quickly in the opening stage. Carlo instructed his national team to ride up front, it was a question of not missing the right breakaway – his riders had to be there for that. But Remco pedalled along at the back of the peloton. What's he up to now, Carlo asked himself. 'I drove up to him,' says the coach. 'And I told him he should be at the front, that's where it was going to happen, not from the back.'

'Yes, coach, yes,' said Remco.
'And I saw him move up towards the front,' says Carlo.
'Just before the top of the climb, a couple of them broke away.'
One was the Italian, the other was Remco.
'I thought: my God, what a guy.'
They gained about a minute's lead, and Bomans was able to follow them in the car. There, while leading in the Trophée Morbihan Juniors, Remco was muttering, complaining, and grumbling: the Italian didn't want to overtake, he'd been behind him for kilometres already, it wasn't on, he didn't want to carry him any longer, he was going to drop him.

'Hang on for another lap yet,' I said. 'It was still too far,' states Carlo.
The Italian national coach drove up alongside Carlo: 'Piano! Piano! Go and tell your guy he should ease off.'

Remco called Carlo back to him: 'Can I drop him now, coach? Can I?'
Carlo thought it was too early – there were so many kilometres still left to ride.
Remco: 'What about now? Can I now?'

They were riding side by side, the young rider and his coach. 'The Italian had to drop back when we were chatting.' The Italian – Andrea Piccolo – was still able to shout something: 'Please, sir! Please, sir!' But yes, Carlo Bomans now says: what can a person do about it? What does a person do about so much class, such a commitment, so great a will? And away he went – Remco won with a lead of minutes.

Carlo Bomans had one more piece of advice for Remco. In the car on the way to the doping check, the coach talked about the teammates. It would be good to conserve them a bit in the final stage, Bomans thought. 'Learn to trust them, they'll get you where you want to be. Then you can go and do your own thing.'

It was now the end of May 2018, and the Belgian championship was being ridden around the Lac de L'Eau d'Heure. With 3 kilometres done, 15 riders had already escaped the peloton. Remco was among them: 'Remco had stepped on it and dragged those riders along with him. But they were all dropped in the next lap,' Carlo recounts. 'He then rode the next 110 kilometres on his own. Remco had become Belgian champion.' Carlo reflects on his way of working at that time. He recounts that as national coach, he started at the front of the race so that he could follow the leading group immediately after a breakaway with his support vehicle. 'That's so I can see what's happening.' In that Belgian championship, he saw Remco gradually pulling further ahead.

Carlo drove alongside Remco.
And said: 'For goodness sake! I'm not going to ride next to that smurf for 100 kilometres, am I?'
Carlo asked Remco: 'How are you feeling?'
Remco answered: 'Good! 'Good!'
Carlo: 'Keep riding at your own pace, Remco. I'm off, we'll see each other again real soon!'
Remco: 'What, coach?'

Carlo: 'Surely you don't think I'm going to drive behind you for all those laps, do you? I'm going to the back, I'm going to watch the race!' Because that's where a real race was going on. For second and third place only it's true, but even so that was an actual contest.

On the final lap, Bomans returned to the lone cyclist.

And asked the question of questions: 'Remco, why do you do that?'

After all, you could have just kept riding around with those 15 guys, couldn't you Remco? You could have also said 'be seeing you guys' two laps before the end, you know? Why, Remco?

Carlo: 'Remco looked at me. He didn't see what the problem was. After all, he'd won, he said.'

It was of course true that Remco had won. But Carlo carried on: 'Remco, that's not racing, man. Riding 100 kilometres on your own, in front, that's not racing. What are you going to do later in the professionals? You won't be able to do that there, ride at the front for all that distance.' Carlo Bomans laughs, knowing that his statement from 2018 quickly became outdated: Remco also rides alone at the front for kilometres in the pro ranks – you know that.

Carlo briefly thinks back to that time, the time when the young man began to scale the heights in 2018: 'The only mistake I made back then was not writing down all the advice I gave Remco – and also his young team mates – or what I told them. That the time of having steak at 6 in the morning was long gone, for example, that those were stories from the past that were occasionally told in the butcher's and the baker's, but that everything was different now, with meticulously planned and carefully considered nutrition. If I'd written all that down back then, it would now, after so many years, be clear that what I had said was indeed the truth.'

It was time for the European championship. On Sunday, 15 July 2018, the race over 118.8 kilometres was started in Brno (Czech Republic) at 9 o'clock in the morning. After the start, there were some cobblestones, then it was up a small hill, followed by a descent, and then a long climb. 'At the foot of that first ascent, four riders broke away, and at the top of the hill, there was only one man riding at the front on his own: that was Remco,' Carlo recounts. Remco quickly gained a 50-second lead, giving Bomans time to approach him in the support vehicle.

Marten de Bruin, the Dutch UCI commissaire, thought it was too early. But Carlo knew Remco, the front-runner, well enough. And said: 'No, Marten, it's not too early. The race is over.' Marten didn't get that: they'd only just completed a small lap, hadn't they? What are you saying now, Carlo? Shouldn't we wait a bit longer, Carlo? Carlo was right: the race was finished, Remco extended his lead, further and further. And still further. He rode the entire race at the front unaccompanied. 'The men in the peloton were no longer going to be involved with whatever Remco was doing there. They opted to ride for the two other medals. Minutes behind Remco, another race within the race was underway.' Remco became – quite simply – European champion on the road. A few days earlier, he had become champion in the time trial. But that was a more difficult job, says Carlo: 'For that he had to work, you know! Getting away from Ilan Van Wilder was no easy task. In the end, it eventually worked out, but no, it didn't happen automatically.'

Fast forward a couple of months, it was now the end of September 2018. The World Championships were held in Salzburg, Austria. On Tuesday, 25 September, Remco won the time trial – by now almost a habit. On Thursday, 27 September, the entire Belgian national team rode in support of him in the road race. 'There was a huge crash,' says Carlo. Remco was involved in it, he didn't immediately have a new wheel, then he switched bikes, lost touch, certainly by nearly 2 minutes – rode up from group to group, eventually ending up in a group with two teammates, who helped him get further forward until Remco was at the head of the race. There he *briefly* had a German in his slipstream, but before long he was off again, on his way to becoming world champion.'

Yep, says Carlo Bomans. 'Should a rider like that, should Remco still be riding among the juniors? Should such a young man, one so passionate and driven, who absorbed everything you told him, everything you passed on to him, who had inherited the nature of his athletic mother and father, and had a physique that could handle all those efforts... Should such a young man carry on racing with the under-23s for another year?' Carlo was uncertain about that at the time: 'Yes, I was concerned about his future. If he were to skip that category, would he burn out too soon? If he were to move up to the professionals, would he end up in a team where he could and would be allowed to ride in the finals, and wouldn't have to be a helper fetching water bottles and rain jackets and then dropping out after 150 kilometres? Because that way, he wouldn't become a cyclist.'

Carlo was sitting with them and he knew there had been discussions about joining Axel Merckx's development team. But he also knew that there had been talks with Patrick Lefevere. They'd seen what kind of results, what kind of values Remco was putting in the tables with the West Flemish manager's team. And so, says Carlo: 'Why should he still have to become an under-23 rider then? With the benefit of hindsight, it was a smart decision to turn professional.'

13

'YOUR CHILD IS
THROWN INTO
THE WORLD OF
ADULTS AT
THAT MOMENT.'

After his interlude in the climb project, with Forte and Acrog-Tormans and with the national junior team, Remco had now become a full-time cyclist. It was more than 18 months since he'd been a footballer. Followers of (international) cycling had watched in amazement at the lightning development of the young man from Schepdaal. Remco was ready for a professional life in the world of cycling – it was now 2019. It was true that he was still only 19 years old. But – and you've already read this in the earlier chapters – there was a broadly shared consensus among the coaches: Remco would not skip any steps by not joining the under-23s, he was simply ready for a place in the elite peloton.

As Carlo Bomans mentioned, there had been talks with Axel Merckx and Patrick Lefevere, that's true. 'It's actually simple,' says his father, Patrick Evenepoel. 'There was an agreement with Merckz and Lefevere.' It was like this: Remco would ride with the development team until Patrick Lefevere deemed he was ready to join the professional team. All parties were able to agree on this; it was a highly acceptable arrangement. But there was an important element at play that invoked a degree of nervousness: Remco's performances during those days of contract negotiations were so overwhelming that (many) other teams sought contact with the young rider's entourage – or at least were attempting to do so. Supposing Merckx and Lefevere hesitated, waited too long to see how things would develop? What if Remco were to move to Axel's under-23 team first? And what if the top teams were to pounce in the meantime? Maybe it would be better, after all, for Remco to immediately ride with the pros. No time for prevaricating, then. Shouldn't that be obvious?

In the end, the decision was made quickly: at the beginning of 2019, Remco would immediately become a professional in Patrick Lefevere's team, and he would no longer take an intermediate step with the under-23s. Remco would ride straight away with Quick Step – then known as Deceuninck-Quick Step. 'Purely in terms of sport, it made no difference,' says Patrick Evenepoel. 'They weren't going to put Remco in the deep end immediately with the pros. They were going to treat him with care.'

That contract with Quick Step was signed in mid-July 2018.
'It was the day when Remco was a guest on *Vive le Vélo*,' says his father Patrick, now more than four years since that particular day. *Vive le Vélo* is the programme on the Flemish public broadcaster – VRT – that accompanies the Tour de France with a refreshing, somewhat playful tone. It's summer, a brief interlude in the daily grind, away from the breakaways, the collapses, the victories, and the disappointments of the stage that has just been ridden. The day is put to rest with a glass of red wine and – often – against the background of a château or a charming village square.

On Wednesday, 18 July, presenter Karl Vannieuwkerke had made himself at home in La Plagne Montalbert. On that day in 2018, the 11th stage had been raced between Albertville and La Rosière, an Alpine stage covering 108.5 kilometres. Welshman Geraint Thomas from Team Sky had won. The next day, the riders would travel from Bourg-Saint-Maurice to Alpe d'Huez. Thomas would win again and on 29 July he would also become the overall winner of the 105th edition of the Tour de France, ahead of Tom Dumoulin and Chris Froome.

There was a chill in the air in La Plagne Montalbert, when the broadcast started late in the evening of 18 July. The sun had disappeared between the mountains, and at an altitude of 1,350 metres a jacket at the outdoor table was welcome. As always in the programme, the surroundings were a picture: alpine meadows, mountains... in short, a taste of holiday on television. There were three guests that evening. The first two were Sven Nys, cyclocross champion and in-house analyst, and Kevin De Weert, whom you already know from his stories earlier in this book.

The third invited guest was Remco Evenepoel.

While he was being introduced by Karl Vannieuwkerke, Remco posed in the setting sun, looking into the camera with a steady gaze. Relaxed, he calmly crossed his arms, his hair was (quite) long, and he was wearing a white T-shirt – perhaps looking a bit bulkier than he does now, in 2024. If you look up the broadcast on the worldwide web, you'll notice a neat detail: Remco already had his own 'brand' printed on the left chest of the jersey – R.EV 1703. Remco was announced as 'a double European champion in the juniors'. That was true of course: just a few days earlier, Remco had been outstanding in the time trial and road race in Brno. Remco had begun to make a name for himself and the press wanted to know more about this young man of just 18 years. It's fantastic to look back at the footage from that time – 18 July 2018 – with the benefit of today's hindsight. Quite simply, Remco made a formidable impression. Karl, Sven, and Kevin watched and listened in admiration to what the rider, who was still a junior at the time, had to say. Somehow or other, Remco radiated a kind of self-assurance, an unshakeable confidence in himself, a kind of inner peace. These may sound like high-flown words, but even so: Remco, the youth, seemed to already know that evening that he – even then, in the depths of his thoughts – was the Remco who would go on to make it in the world of professional cycling. And these too are words on a similar level: Remco seemed to enjoy an element of authority at the table of *Vive le Vélo*. The presenter and the two other (older) guests were, in a positive way, overwhelmed.

'How does it affect you when everyone labels you as a phenomenon, an exceptional talent? It's hard to deal with that, I think,' said Karl Vannieuwkerke. Remco's answer was mature – it can't be described any other way: 'Gosh, yes,' he said, unfazed. 'I've already heard so many good comments by now. I think that hearing this is pretty normal for me at the moment. But it should always be understood that I haven't really proven anything yet – well, on my level with the juniors, perhaps – but in the cycling world, that still doesn't mean anything. What I mean to say is, in the pros, everything starts again from zero, and they won't be looking back at what I achieved at the European Championships or in the weeks before them. So there's still a long road ahead, and with the pros, it's only just beginning.'

It's no exaggeration to say: Karl, Sven and Kevin were *flabbergasted*. Flabbergasted? Is that the closest way of putting it? It most probably is: the three men around the table appeared to be stunned by the degree of insight. But if you examine the footage closely – and it's well worth doing so – you'll see that Remco himself was completely at ease when he spoke the words. There sat a young man who knew what he was doing. Karl, the host, answered: 'I have to say, Remco, that's a great first answer for a first appearance on a talk show. That too will go well.' Remco laughed, briefly. It was the laugh of someone who had all their ducks in a row – I know for sure that it will go well, he must have thought.

The memories that Patrick Evenepoel has of that programme are a match with the truth. That evening, after 6 minutes and 39 seconds on the talk show, Remco indeed revealed the news that he would become a professional cyclist with Patrick Lefevere on 1 January 2019. He added that 'it was indeed early days.' The reason? Remco went on to say: Sky had come up with an enormous offer, and Quick Step immediately jumped on it and said, "No, he's under our wing," and they wanted to secure that right away.' It was a two-year contract with an option for two more years. Remco would undoubtedly feel good in the team, he said. After all, he'd already been in contact with riders like Yves Lampaert and Iljo Keisse, he'd already participated in a training camp with them in Calpe, and he felt it was a family with whom he already felt at home. The plan was to focus on climbing and time trials – 'That's where my strengths lie,' said Remco. Plus: 'And I have the ability to recover from them.' In short and in his own words, 'to develop into a stage rider. 'I dream of doing well in the three Grand Tours.'

Karl Vannieuwkerke pitched in and immediately pointed out a danger lurking round the corner: the immense pressure from the media. Remco didn't take the bait; he remained calm and simply stated that he knew he still had a long way to go. Don't worry about it, he seemed to imply. And, Sven Nys said: 'I got to know the parents for a day, they were the first coaches, and I think they've done a great job up to this point. And when you see how down-to-earth they are, I think that's a good sign. It's particularly important to keep both feet on the ground, to keep doing your own thing, and not let yourself be driven crazy. Because, indeed, they will quickly praise you to the heavens. But when things aren't going so well, they will just as quickly knock you down again.'

There sat Remco, on television for the very first time, speaking about his own career for the first time, his own dreams, and his own expectations. All at once, Patrick and Agna realised that they'd become the parents of a professional cyclist – was it not a bit too early, too fast? Agna had some doubts as her son was still so young. Patrick ponders for a moment and then says: 'Our child was hurled into an adult world at that moment.' Reminiscing, he says: 'Remco couldn't be considered a child, given the intense way he approached football as well. No, even then you couldn't call him a child. We often had comments from Anderlecht and PSV that we shouldn't keep Remco at it so obsessively. But we weren't doing that. People always thought that we were pushing him hard, but it wasn't like that. Remco decided that for himself, he wanted all of it, it came from within him. And that made a huge difference: if that tenacity comes from your child himself, then it can succeed. If it's the parents that want it, it fails. Remco wanted it. Remco wants it.'

Patrick, after pausing: 'What happened to Remco was a first. There was no precedent for a rider skipping the under-23 category.

14

'WE DON'T KNOW
EACH OTHER,
BUT I'LL TAKE
CARE OF YOUR
SON AS THOUGH
HE WERE MY
OWN CHILD.'

For a few years in the mid-1970s, Patrick Lefevere was a professional cyclist, first with Ebo-Cinzia (in that nostalgic green-black jersey), then with Ebo-Superia and Marc Zeepcentrale-Superia. He won Gullegem Koerse (you will come across this race later in the book), Kuurne-Brussels-Kuurne, and a stage in the 1978 Tour of Spain. Patrick's career as a rider was over by 1979, when he was still only 24 years old. Very quickly thereafter, he launched his impressive career as a team leader and manager. To start with he was an assistant to Walter Godefroot, and then he became the man in charge of teams that, while frequently changing names at regular intervals as one sponsor left to be replaced by another, always bore (and bear) the stamp of Patrick Lefevere.

'What kind of manager am I?' Patrick Lefevere leans back in his chair in the office of Soudal-Quick-Step's service centre, just after the 2024 season. Before long, in just a couple of weeks, the hustle and bustle will return in full force; right now, his staff are busy with trucks, bikes, and other equipment – they are making sure the housekeeping is in good order before winter begins, and the start of the new season will soon be approaching. Patrick sips his can of soft drink. He ponders for a moment and then says: 'A caring boss, I hope.' And he continues: 'A caring boss, yes. Someone who, among his workers, is one of the most important components of a team. Someone who can get on with his champions. And someone who can bring in the money for the team as well, that's actually my most challenging task.'

Patrick does of course know Matxin, the Basque having worked for Lefevere in 2017. It's true that the talent scout approached his boss/manager about Remco. 'He was always sniffing around, always on the lookout for new talent.' But, Patrick adds: 'I'd already been tipped off by Carlo Bomans about that boy who could ride his bike so fast. I knew Carlo well and still have a good relationship with him. His wife and my wife still often WhatsApp each other. Photos from the past and such.' Carlo was a loyal soldier in Patrick Lefevere's ranks. He was a respected rider – his achievements have already been mentioned above. Later on, Carlo became the national coach, as you know,' Patrick recounts. 'Carlo had the habit of never bothering me, he wasn't someone who would phone me up just for the sake of it. But then, one day, he did just that.'

'I need to bother you for once, Patrick', Carlo had said.
Carlo opened his story as follows:
'I've just seen a *rare bird*, Patrick.'
'This guy has only been racing a few weeks, he hasn't competed in many races as yet.
'He's just started with the juniors,' Carlo had said.
'If he doesn't crash, he rides everyone into the ground.'
'His name is Remco Evenepoel.'
Carlo finished off the phone conversation, saying, 'I wouldn't think about it for too long, Patrick.'

Patrick Lefevere quickly made up his mind: 'I wanted to sign up Remco just as quickly as possible. Because it's not often you find someone like that riding around before he's discovered. Plus: Matxin had also seen him riding, there in the Basque Country. Did I still hesitate? Because he'd only just quit football? Nope. If Carlo phones and if Matxin brings a kid like that to my attention, then I don't hesitate.' No, Patrick didn't get in his car to watch Remco in his next race. He did something else: he invited Mr and Mrs Evenepoel for a chat. Me, Patrick and Agna, sat down in a bistro at Zellik station,' relates Patrick Lefevere. 'I've heard *this, that, and the other* about your son, about Remco,' Patrick had said. And then went on to add: 'He's good, apparently.' That was the point at which the caring, human manager side of Patrick Lefevere kicked in. Patrick had then said: I think we need to take good care of your son because from now on he'll get all kinds of people knocking on the door, even worse than it is in football.' Patrick Lefevere adds in 2024: 'Of course, the father, Patrick had raced himself and he knew a bit about that world. Or no: he knew that world a bit too well.' Patrick Lefevere and Patrick Evenepoel didn't really know each other. Their paths hadn't crossed in the past and they were, in fact, strangers to one another. 'But I told him and his wife that I would look after their son as though he were my own child. If they entrusted him to me, then I would do all in my power to achieve the goals we would set. If Remco turned into a great cyclist, *tant mieux,* so much the better. If it didn't work out, we would still remain good friends,' Lefevere says.

Patrick Lefevere was renowned as a discoverer and coach of top cyclists. Off the cuff, these are the young men who made a name for themselves at a young age at the side of the manager: Fabian Cancellara, Filippo Pozzato, Bernhard Eisel and 'all those guys from Mapei, we had about 40 good riders back then. That team was so good that Hein Verbruggen, the boss of UCI, made me split it into two teams,' says Patrick. There was the period of Klein Constantia, the development team where Julian Alaphilippe, Enric Mas, Rémi Cavagna, and Maximilian Schachmann came to maturity. He can't deny it: yes, there was some jealousy at that time; those Lefevere teams were indeed very good. 'I became seriously ill during that period, life is not always a bed of roses, and that goes for everyone. I then moved for a while to Domo-Farm Frites, where I also set up a youth team. When I returned to Quick-Step, another youth team was established, and I always allowed the humane, caring side of my leadership to come into play.' Sometimes it was a bit of a balancing act, Lefevere says (and in fact, it still is to this day). 'There's been some jealousy among the coaches and the parents of those young guys who offer themselves or to whom I pay more than usual attention. Sometimes I have to disappoint people, that's how it goes. Not everyone is going to make it in the world of cycling. But I always try to make honest choices.' However, such a choice weighs heavily on those close to the young cyclists: parents, brothers and sisters, aunts and uncles don't enjoy hearing that their pride and joy is not good enough. 'On one occasion, a father and son sat in front of me, at this very table. When I told them that the boy's story was at an end, the tears came from both son and father. I completely understood that. Because when the son's dream ends, so too does the family's dream. At the weekend, such a family is busy supporting their son, their grandson, the aspiring cyclist. In the blink of an eye, that's in ruins; in an instant, I take that away. I understand those tears. A year later, I saw the son and his father again. In the meantime, the young man had done well in the company where he worked and had risen to be head of his department. Those people were grateful to me for the decision I'd made for them 12 months earlier.'

After Patrick Lefevere had met Remco Evenepoel's mum and dad, he felt optimistic. 'I already knew from the tests that had been submitted that Remco scored well. There was a strong motor in that youngster. But when I met Patrick and Agna, I noticed straight away that Remco had inherited good genes: his father had been a cyclist, and his mother looked very athletic. She had been an outstanding volleyball player, so Remco had that DNA in him. In short: if he was a mix of his parents, there was a lot of potential in him. I had a good feeling about these people. And presumably they felt the same about me.' In the meantime, Remco rode his next races in the junior category, doing so in an increasingly impressive manner. Patrick Lefevere knew that by now as well. 'The way in which he raced, the way in which he rode away. Yeah.' But the manager had also been struck by something else: 'If he was beaten, Remco could really sulk about it. Have you ever seen that photo? When he lost to Girmay in the sprint? He could really get annoyed, that was just the reality. But in the meantime Remco has learned how to deal with that.' Patrick had noticed that: Not only did Remco have the legs of a champion but he also had the mind of a winner. He ponders for a moment: 'A good head? What is that? It's hard to explain. I've worked with a lot of champions, they do have something special, it's true.'

Patrick Lefevere produces an analysis, examining three generations. 'In the 1990s, Johan Museeuw was introverted towards the outside world and kept it at bay. He said little about his ambitions. But he did make them come true. Johan just did it. In the 2000s along came Tom Boonen. With his rich Kempen accent, Tom was a good talker. He knew what he was capable of but did not brag about it. At the same time, he was not afraid to be the team leader. And Tom won. Now, in the 2020s, we have

Remco. Remco says in advance what he's going to do, but until recently, people thought that was boasting. "Shouldn't you learn to pedal first," people would say. As you know, people are like that, they can be unkind. They enjoy it, giving criticism. They enjoy seeing when something goes wrong. But Remco answered them through the pedals. Did you watch him in action at the Olympic Games? I watched it at home from my sofa, I didn't feel like driving to Paris in all that commotion. I saw it all happen there, two weekends in a row, him at the age of 24. Is he still going to improve? Yes, Remco will still improve. Not so spectacularly as over the past few years, that's not possible. But, little by little, his experience will come into play and he will become even stronger. It will now be about the fine-tuning.'

Returning to the first conversations between Patrick and the Evenepoel family...

Patrick Lefevere would let Remco develop for a year with Axel Merckx's development team. 'The Evenepoel family then went to look at the equipment with Axel and his father Eddy.' But alarm bells soon started ringing for Lefevere. 'Of course, I wasn't the only one who saw the feats Remco was pulling off on the bike, no one had seen anything like it before, no one could ignore all those victories. *That couldn't go unnoticed.* And suddenly, those other teams – like Sky and so on – started flashing amounts that couldn't be compared to what I was spending at the time. I knew I had to be careful. *Uh-oh*, I thought. This could turn out badly,' relates the manager. Patrick Lefevere gave Remco a contract for two years. Eddy and Axel Merckx didn't like it at all – they were pissed, in Patrick's words.

'But yeah, it was either that or losing him,' says Patrick.
And thus Remco became a professional.
'That went reasonably well to start with,' relates manager Lefevere.
'And then it was time for the Tour of Belgium.

Remco was riding so hard there that Victor Campenaerts almost blacked out, causing him to fall on the bend. On that day, Remco won his first stage. I gave him a bonus then even though it wasn't in his contract.'

'He also won in San Sebastián that year.'

Patrick Lefevere laughs, takes a sip of his cola and says: 'I then changed Remco's contract. I put *a zero* after the amount.'

15

'IT RAINED AND
RAINED AND RAINED.
AND THEN HE HAD TO
GO FOR A PEE. HE GOT
ANGRY AND SENT A
MESSAGE: "MAKE SURE
YOU'RE AT THE FINISH
LINE IN ZOTTEGEM
TOMORROW. YOU'RE
IN FOR A SURPRISE,
MUM AND DAD."'

From 12 to 16 June 2019, the Tour of Belgium was held between Sint-Niklaas and Beringen. It wasn't a particularly difficult race, with two flat stages, two hilly stages, and a short time trial in between. Remco showed what he was capable of. After those five days through his homeland, the cycling world – once again – was left gasping: 'How did that youngster do it?'

The first stage from Sint-Niklaas to Knokke-Heist, over a distance of 183.5 kilometres, was expected to be right up their street for the sprinters and their teams. The expectation was that riders like Tim Merlier, Arne Marit, Bryan Coquard, Tom Van Asbroeck, and Jasper Philipsen would fight it out among themselves in the bunch sprint for the stage win. In addition to those fast riders, there was another cyclist that the followers were taking into account: Fabio Jakobsen, the Deceuninck-Quick Step sprinter and thus Remco's teammate. But in that first stage, there was no sprint finish. The Dutchman Jan-Willem van Schip – the rather headstrong road cyclist cum track rider with his specially mounted small handlebars on his bike and his often hilarious and wide-ranging interviews after a race – had escaped. This wasn't a problem per se, with every stage in a race featuring the escape of the day. But this is always caught a few kilometres from the finish, with the sprinter teams being able to count on that. At least: that's what usually happens. But, in the first stage of the Tour of Belgium, that wasn't the case: Jan-Willem stayed beyond the reach of the onrushing peloton, as it's usually so nicely expressed in cycling language. He won with a 4-second lead over Merlier, Jakobsen, Lionel Taminiaux, Roy Jans, Philipsen, Daan Soete, Van Asbroeck, Marit, and Rudy Barbier – the sprinters of the day, who had miscalculated. Or better said: it was their teams that had done the miscalculating. Also, Deceuninck-Quick Step, who was working for Fabio Jakobsen, had not been able to fight its way back onto Jan-Willem's wheel. Afterwards, there was resentment within Jakobsen and Remco's team: how come they hadn't been able to close that final gap – Van Schip was only 50 metres in front of them? Team leader Rik Van Slycke was mainly angry at Remco. Something had occurred to Rik during the race: along the

Expressway to Knokke, the peloton had been stretched out in a long line. It rained, and rained, and rained. They were racing hard, the pace was intense.

And then one rider disappeared from the line.
He had stopped in that bad weather.
And went and stood at the side.
It rained and rained and rained.
The rider had to take a pee.
The rider in question was Remco.
'He'll never make it back into the peloton,' was the immediate response. Such speed and such bad weather: 'He won't be coming back.'
Plus: 'Why is he doing that now? At a time like this?'
The bottom line was that Remco ought to have understood better that he needed to race as part of the team ranks. Rik believed that this had not happened, or at least insufficiently. Remco experienced the conversation with Rik as unpleasant, surprising, and a bit threatening. Perhaps the young rider – who was of course still finding his way – felt a bit uncomfortable with that. But at the same time, Remco also showed the resilience that would become – or rather, already was – so typical of him.

Remco was angry, says his father Patrick. 'And in the evening he sent us, his parents, a message. The message said that we should make sure we were present at the finish of the second stage, in Zottegem. There, he would show us something, he wrote.' That second stage, over 179.9 kilometres, became a race that will undoubtedly earn a prominent place in *the books on Remco Evenepoel's rich cycling career*. Because Remco did what he had already done so often in the past two years: he broke away from the peloton. One person accompanied him: Victor Campenaerts. Victor is known as a thoroughbred hard rider, a man who eats up kilometres. On 16 April 2019, Campenaerts had become the world hour record holder 2 months before the second stage of the Tour of Belgium. In short: Remco had the ideal man by his side in his attempt to win the stage in Zottegem. But Remco rode hard, emphatically hard. So hard that Victor was forced into a mistake. At 6.7 kilometres from the finish line, the two of them found themselves in a left-hand bend. Remco was in front with Campenaerts sat in his wheel, on what was a slightly hollow road between the Flemish fields, with a culvert on the right and a concrete wall. The two of them had a 38-second lead on the first pursuers, with the peloton trailing by 1'17".

This is the transcript from the Flemish public broadcaster's live reporting. The reporters were Sven Nys and Christophe Vandegoor. This is what they said:

'Campenaerts has come off! He's slipping off the road! Just when it couldn't get worse!' (about Victor)

At the very limit! Pushing beyond it! Anything to stay in touch with that wheel.' (about Victor)

'He's off, completely on his own! (about Remco)

'There's no holding him back now.' (about Remco)

'Just look at the pace he's developing...' (about Remco)

'Purely from his own strength. Into attack mode. All done on his own.' (about Remco)

On 13 June 2019, Remco won his first race among elite riders. In Zottegem, he had a 42-second lead over the sprinting peloton. His teammate Fabio Jakobsen took second. Agna and Patrick were standing by the finish line, having done what their son had asked them to in the message the night before. He had, in turn, kept his promise: 'I'll show you something.' Three days later, he became the overall winner of the Tour of Belgium. It's appropriate here to revisit the words Jef Robert said a few chapters back. He said there that Remco had enormous drive and cast-iron determination, and that he showed no trace of fear of failure. What he accomplished in the Tour of Belgium was clear evidence of that. Robert also said that Remco would push harder whenever he received criticism. That was also apparent in the Tour of Belgium.

His father, Patrick, has often reflected on those days in June 2019. Whether these events indicate that his son has a bad character? No, that's not the case. OK, it's true that Remco is tough in the race and doesn't back down, even towards team managers. But such things are part and parcel of a rider. And though it might seem a bit selfish, it's not wrong to stand your ground, especially at the highest level – and that's where Remco was aiming to be. Isn't it true after all that athletes – men and women – who strive to reach the top in their discipline are tough, both on others and on themselves? 'And don't forget,' says Patrick, 'that a career can progress fast. New talents can appear before you know it. In the time trial, Remco took on riders like Rohan Dennis, who was a bit older, and Filippo Ganna, who was closer in age to Remco. All of them were battling for their position and for the medals at the championships. There's nothing wrong with directly fighting your own corner. Just think about this: Remco is still only 24 years old, and yet is already someone coming in as a great prospect to compete with the big names: In the 2023 World Time Trial Championships, Joshua Tarling came third, no less. In short, there's no time to lose, the years go by faster than you think.'

However, Patrick wants to add something to this: While Remco may be tough in the race, he isn't like that in normal life. For example, he experienced almost childlike excitement when Lobke Spinoy became Flemish champion. Lobke is a member of the Academy – you'll read more about that later. 'Remco was sitting in the Dauphiné,' says Patrick. 'That's where he heard Lobke's fantastic news. Then he posts it on his social media. That girl was in seventh heaven. Remco thinks that's cool.'

On Sunday 30 June 2019, two weeks after his victory in the Tour of Belgium, the Belgian Road Championship for elite riders took place over a distance of 223.8 kilometres. Tim Merlier – who was still a full-time cyclocross rider at the time and racing for Corendon-Circus – won the bunch sprint ahead of Timothy Dupont and Wout van Aert (who was still referred to as 'the cyclocross rider' in the coverage at that time). It was a fascinating race, in full sun, first through the Zwalm region, and later around the Blaarmeersen area in Ghent. That Tim Merlier won was surprising – he was actually new to the road peloton and was still finding his feet. The title of Belgian champion was a real boost for him and paved the way for the career he went on to build, with stage victories in the Grand Tours, a new Belgian title, and – the pinnacle of his achievements – the European title in 2024, once again in a bunch sprint.

But it was another rider who was the main topic of conversation on 30 June: Remco. He left everyone speechless again. This is what happened. After the ride through the Flemish Ardennes, when the peloton had settled down, Remco made his move. He was accompanied by Dries De Bondt (from Corendon-Circus) and Jelle Wallays and Stan Dewulf (both from Lotto-Soudal). Reporter Michel Wuyts and former rider José De Cauwer provided commentary on the live broadcast on Flemish public television. What was immediately noticeable: a massive crowd had gathered for the race, with people standing in crowded rows. What also stood out: the admiration during the broadcast for Remco's exploits.

This is what Michel and José were saying, cutting in on each other, live on air...
'There goes Remco!'
'Oh, oh, oh!!'
'There goes Evenepoel!'
'And now De Bondt is pulling out all the stops. Using short, sharp bursts, he's trying to close the gap. But he's not really in full flow up at the front.'
'The locomotive has left the station.'
'Dewulf, he's dropping off.'
'Is it now up to De Bondt to catch up?'
'He's already made up a good 30 metres.'
'Now let's see what he can do on the bends. His ability to pick up speed? I don't doubt it.'

The director showed the peloton on screen, with the chasing teams working to close the gap, which remained at 42 seconds for a long time. Slogging away, in the full sun.

Back to the front of the race...

'What has happened at the front?'

'They're tucked in behind his wheel. It's De Bondt that's pulled that off.'

'Yes.'

'That was painful.'

'We've lost Dewulf.'

'The question is: will those men continue to stay in touch...?'

'Gosh, why not?'

'They've committed to this challenge, all they can do now is keep on riding.'

There were still 31.9 kilometres to go, with the lead measuring 39 seconds. Remco was riding hard at the front, with the other two following in his slipstream. Remco indicated with his elbow – 'Come on, take over'.

'There's no immediate changeover.'

'Just like Victor Campenaerts in the Tour of Belgium, it's now their turn to experience the speed at which that young man rides...'

'No one is getting past, for now.'

Renaat Schotte, the man on the motorbike, came in the middle of the race and intervened...

'Evenepoel is engaged in a bit of diplomacy.'

Remco dropped back to third position; he wanted to talk with his fellow breakaway riders. But De Bondt and Wallays – experienced pros – didn't respond. 'Wallays blatantly looked the other way,' said Renaat. The stragglers crossed the finish line – they had now raced for 4 hours, 19 minutes, and 30 seconds. Wuyts and De Cauwer saw it all unfold from their booth.

'Wallays will be thinking: compared to me, that one is still a little kid.'

'Just how fast can that little guy ride already?'

'I also spoke about that with Eddy Merckx this week.'

'Nineteen years old! You cannot be serious!'

'Nineteen years old!!'

'19!'

'Merckx won San Remo at the tender age of 20...'
'And finished second in this Belgian Championship in Vilvoorde, behind Walter Godefroot, when he was just 20.' That was in 1965.

The commentators switched back to Renaat...
'He's cranking up the pace again. But are the others willing to do their bit? Yes! At last, De Bondt takes over. Also great to experience the public's enthusiasm. Remco Evenepoel is captured for eternity by his girlfriend on her smart phone. The Remco phenomenon!' And then Schotte uttered his prophetic words: 'Perhaps what they're seeing here is just a taste of what is to come in the next few years.'

Wuyts takes over...
'You're absolutely spot on there.'

As you know, the breakaway ultimately failed to succeed and a bunch sprint took place.
Remco was (still) not Belgian champion. But not to worry, that would come later: in 2022 in the time trials, in 2023 on the road.

After that Belgian Championship in Ghent, Remco's first professional year was by no means over. He went on to become the European champion in the time trials. And he won the Clásica San Sebastián, a true classic, about which you can read more in the next chapter. Remco was the youngest rider ever to win a race at World Tour level. In 2019, Remco became Sports Personality of the Year in Belgium, something he will be honoured by more than once in the years after.

16

'HERE IT IS, SAY THE ARGENTINIANS! LOOK, THEY SAY, WE'VE GOT A PHOTO OF REMCO!'

Some riders aren't that phased about having to contend with a 'comeback'; in fact, they don't experience it as some kind of punishment but rather as a distinctly pleasant phenomenon. What's the story? They enjoy racing in events they've already competed in: because they won there, because they liked the scenery, the food, the atmosphere, the time of year. Remco must have that too, races that he enjoys riding. The Tour of San Juan in Argentina and the Tour of Algarve in Portugal are such races. They take place early in the season and they're ideal for building up form. It's very simple, says Patrick Evenepoel: 'If Remco rode well there, then he goes back there.' And further: 'These races suit his profile, his identity as a rider. They're races with a nice mix of a time trial, some tough stages, and a few easier ones.' These are races where you sometimes have to keep pushing hard, where high wattages can be generated. Plus: in the Algarve, the distances between locations are minimal, and teams don't need to move at all or not that much from hotel to hotel after completing stages. Then again, it's different in San Juan, where the Tour is also a challenging and beautiful one, with top-class riders. 'Then they spend four hours at a time in a van on their way to a rest stop,' says Patrick. 'And they're far from luxurious, those vans, not at all. Then they get dressed for the start while sitting on a plastic garden chair, on a terrace. That too is what top cyclists have to endure. Check it out on YouTube.' In 2024, the Tour of San Juan disappeared from the international cycling calendar and continued as a local competition, with a smaller budget, smaller teams, less prestige.

One day the Evenepoel family received a telephone call. The call emanated from Monchique, Portugal. The people from the village's local council had an announcement to make: there was going to be a statue of Remco at the Alto da Foia. On that climb, Remco had won the mountain stage of the Tour of Algarve on 20 February 2020. He then immediately became leader of the overall classification as well, a position he would not relinquish. On 23 February, Remco became the overall winner, succeeding Tadej Pogačar on the honours list – in the Algarve too, it's mostly the best riders who win. The announcement from the council came as a surprise; no one in Remco's entourage was aware of the plans, and they had managed to keep it well hidden in Portugal. And so, Remco now has a statue; it depicts the victory gesture that he made on 20 February 2020. That is remarkable. Cyclists are often honoured with a statue, but usually closer to home – a bust in the market square of the village where they were born, where they messed around as kids and rode their first laps around the church. It's more common to honour cyclists with a statue after their career, when they are quite a bit older. Remco was not old, he was still very young when his chiselled likeness appeared in the form of a statue on the Alto da Foia. People already hold Remco in adoration, something his family experiences firsthand in Schepdaal. Sometimes fans timidly walk into the coffee shop next to the church. Then they look around for a bit, finger the T-shirts and jerseys with pictures of Remco, ask if Patrick is his father, and order an espresso. Sometimes they let on that they are from Argentina – 'Look,' they say, 'a photo of Remco.' And Patrick sees his son, with – indeed – the people now sitting with him having coffee. They are beaming in the photo and they're beaming in real life – Patrick finds it endearing and says: 'That's the sport for you, the cyclists are so approachable for the people, they are so close to their supporters, Later in this book, Patrick and Agna will return to the status their son has already earned.

A race that Remco is very eager to return to is the Clásica San Sebastián. The classic in the Basque Country takes place a week after the end of the Tour de France – often, the strong riders from the Tour extend their peak condition by participating in the Clásica, which is called the Donostia-Donostia Klasikoa in Basque. The race is not really old, not a classic in the true sense of the word. But it's a race that every good rider wants to win – it looks impressive on the *palmares* or list of achievements. For the record, a list of winners' names: Miguel Indurain, Adri van der Poel, Claude Criquielion, Gianni Bugno, Claudio Chiappucci, Alejandro Valverde, Luis Leon Sanchez, Philippe Gilbert. The critical factor in the race is usually the Jaikibel, a hill near the sea and not particularly high, barely 450 metres. But it's climbed twice, and the race becomes jittery, with the first attacks being launched. After the descent, the Alto de Arkale follows, and – to add some extra spice to the Clásica – the Alto de Murgil, just 7 kilometres from the finish. Sprinters don't often win in San Sebastián.

Remco has won there on no less than three occasions so far: in 2019, his first professional year and again in both 2022 and 2023. 'The roads around San Sebastián are suited to Remco,' says Patrick. But surely there's more to it than that? The next paragraph presents the beginning of an answer.

There's another race that really suits Remco: Liège-Bastogne-Liège, La Doyenne, the oldest classic there is, one of the five Monuments, the others being Milan-San Remo, Tour of Flanders, Paris-Roubaix, and Tour of Lombardy. Tough and often cold, with Ardennes climbs whose names resound like bells: La Redoute, Stockeu, Côte de Wanne, Col du Rosier, Côte des Forges, La Roche-aux-Faucons, Côte de la Haute-Levée, and many more. The men who win in Liège are men in the true sense of the word, the best riders of their day. Familiar names, all of them, they belong to the all-time greats: Roger De Vlaeminck and Jacques Anquetil, Dietrich Thurau and Fred De Bruyne, Moreno Argentin and Stan Ockers, Ferdy Kübler and Walter Godefroot, Bernard Hinault and Rik Van Looy. And – five times! – Eddy Merckx, of course. Riders from the hall of fame. More recently, Tadej Pogačar won twice, in 2021 and 2024. Remco won in 2022 and 2023. Why is the Ardennes classic's course so perfectly suited to Remco? Patrick Evenepoel doesn't have to contemplate for very long before coming up with an answer to that question: 'Remco is purely and simply the type of rider who relies on his great stamina. Remco is a rider suited to long and tough climbs, like those you get in Liège and San Sebastián. In the Tour of Flanders, the climbs are more suited to fast-twitch types. The Kwaremont, just to give an example, will suit Remco less. Should he apply himself to that? I don't think so, really. Remco will apply himself to pursuing his big dream: winning the three Grand Tours. The Tour and the Giro are still there on his to-do list, something everyone in the world of cycling is fully aware of.' Patrick adds a few more words to that: 'Remco would prefer to win those Grand Tours with his current team, Soudal-Quick-Step.' Keep those words in mind, for we'll need to return to them again in this book.

Remco has already ticked off the Vuelta – the third Grand Tour – from his list.
That happened in 2022.

17

'NO, I'M
NEVER GOING TO
EXPERIENCE A
YEAR LIKE THIS
AGAIN. IT CAN'T
GET ANY BETTER.'

In the meantime, Remco had secured a strong, prominent position at the head of the elite peloton. There were magnificent victories and times too when things didn't go as smoothly. That was, of course, still quite natural – after all, he was still just a 20-year-old, a relative youngster. In this chapter, we provide a whistle-stop tour of the years that followed Remco's debut as a professional in 2019. In 2020, Remco got the new season off to a start by heading to the Tour of San Juan. He proved his not insignificant ability for time trials once again: he won the (short) race against the clock. That was the immediate building block for his overall victory in the Argentine stage race. Obviously, Remco also won the young rider classification. If you look at the results Remco recorded between 2020 and the end of 2024, you'll notice that he won the young rider classification almost everywhere, including in the Tour de France – and by 2024, Remco had already been a professional cyclist for five years. Not only is it proof of Remco's outstanding performances, but also of his unbelievably young age: Remco was a youth of nineteen when he became a rider in the elite category.

In 2020, Remco won stages and the overall classification in the Tour of the Algarve, stages and the overall classification in the Tour of Burgos and in the Tour of Poland. That was no mean achievement – on the contrary. Meanwhile, coronavirus had the world in its grip. And then Saturday, 15th August came around, when the drama of Lombardy unfolded. Here, we want to take a brief look at that day again, this time viewed from the perspective of Patrick Lefevere, the team manager.

'There I was, in Luca Paolini's coffee shop. We were following the stage on television. Patrick and Agna were present, as was Oumi. Alessandro Tegner, the communications manager, and Stephanie Clerckx, the PR and media assistant, were there watching the race too. I'm fluent in Italian, so I could follow everything that was being said perfectly well. Suddenly I heard it said: *C'è la bici di Evenepoel.* I recognised that voice, it was the deep voice of the man on the motorbike during the race. Among the team, we called him 'Il commissario'. There's Evenepoel's bike. There's Remco's bike! I was thinking: if that's his bike, then where's Remco? Has he swapped perhaps? Remco had dropped off slightly from the leading group on that descent, by some 10 or 20 metres. Had he experienced a difficult moment? Was it a slight hunger dip? In any case: Vincenzo Nibali had noticed it and started descending *full gas*. Nibali was one of the best downhill riders in the peloton, if not the very best. And, what also influenced him: he wasn't happy about the arrival of that little *johnny-come-lately*. Remco was a threat to the established names. So Nibali wanted to lose him, there in the descent. Remco must have misjudged that bend, he *walloped* that wall.' Patrick and company saw the footage, and suddenly there was complete consternation – Oumi had gone outside, she was being comforted, and chilling moments followed.

'I thought to myself, says Patrick, 'I don't want to see a repetition of that footage of Fabio Casartelli, that youngster who died on the Col de Portet d'Aspet, in the descent during the 1995 Tour, with a distraught Johan Museeuw beside him, there on that road. I didn't want that. But Remco was lying in that ravine, and I just hoped there were some bushes there that might have broken his fall. I hoped there were trees, maybe Remco had ended up among them. But there weren't any, behind that wall it was just a vertical drop below. Something happened inside Patrick Lefevere then, something that always happens to him in extreme situations: he became calm and started thinking ahead. 'Whenever a crisis strikes, I immediately think three times faster, I think three steps ahead. I don't know how it works, but it does.' Patrick thought, then: 'If they look down with the camera now, into the ravine, there's a chance it won't look good at all. How am I going to respond to the people around me, Remco's loved ones? How am I going to deal with this?' Patrick saw on the footage that Remco was moving, the team directors Davide Bramati and Geert Van Bondt wanted to go down, but there was no path, it was just a sheer drop below. 'There was no doctor, he had driven on past, the support vehicles having only seen the bike leaning against the wall. A stretcher needed to be brought to the scene of the accident, but that was no simple matter. I asked Luca Paolini which was the best clinic in the area. I phoned it but there was no answer, no response. We drove there and arrived before the ambulance. There we waited until they finally arrived.'

Patrick Lefevere pauses for a second.
'That's where Remco saw his family,' he says then.
'They held him.'
'They gave him a hug.'
'Then Remco began to sob,' recounts Lefevere.
Patrick looks straight ahead and says: 'Do you know what Remco said then?'
'Remco said: "Sorry."'
Remco apologised for his fall, for the inconvenience, for not having fought on to the end for victory.
Patrick: 'All we could say was: "Don't say sorry, Remco. You've done nothing wrong."'
'I added to that: "We're glad you're with us. We're glad you're still with us."

'Our doctor, José Ibarguren – we call him Doki, little doctor, because he's not very tall. Did father Evenepoel tell him that? – he wasn't allowed in at first, but then eventually he was,' says Lefevere. 'They stabilised Remco, took X-rays, and it took an eternity for those to be ready, at least five times longer than would have been the case in Belgium. Remco had a fractured pelvis, but they hadn't seen the internal bleeding. We had to leave Remco behind. I arranged a hotel for the family. I looked into whether Remco could be flown home by private plane, but that wasn't allowed; it was too soon.

Patrick decides: 'In the end, he was able to go to Herentals. And then began the recovery. Remco was 20 years old and it could have been the end of the road. Or the beginning of the end of the road. But he got himself back together. Isn't that right?'

Toon Claes is an eminent doctor. A highly renowned sports surgeon. At AZ Herentals, he has developed his department into the place of choice for elite athletes to come from all over the world after a fall or injury. His sons, Steven and Tom, work as orthopedic surgeons in the same department as their father. The doctor was watching television that 15th of August, saw the accident happen and what he saw on the screen struck a note with him – 'I got angry, it all took so long before the emergency services arrived. Where on earth are they?' I paid attention directly to the details, on how they started moving Remco, how they treated the victim.' He knew immediately that this wasn't good. At first, Dr Claes followed the events through the media. After the emergency admission to the hospital in Italy and the flight (eventually) back to Belgium, Remco came under his care in Herentals. 'We had already been in touch with the team and the team doctor in Italy. All the communication was handled very well. In other words, we already had some idea of what was going on. 'The transport options were gone into and the practicalities were sorted out,' says Dr Claes. 'So we knew what to expect.' This was – in summary form – the verdict, the diagnosis: Remco had sustained a lung injury, a pelvic fracture, and a pubic bone fracture, the latter of which did not greatly concern the doctor initially.

What exactly does a pubic bone fracture entail? 'In principle, it's not really a life-threatening injury,' says the surgeon. 'It's an injury that will typically heal without an operation, provided the patient gets enough rest. The pubic bone consists of 2 branches, an upper and a lower one. The lower branch of the pubic bone is what humans, and especially cyclists, sit on. Remco had sustained a fracture immediately adjacent to the part of the pelvis you sit on. A fracture here calls for rest. If you neglect to take that rest and, for example, cycle for hours at a time prematurely, the impact can be significant. That bone comes under heavy stress during cycling.

Back to Remco's fall. That these were the only fractures he'd sustained from this type of fall was actually surprising. 'For a fall like that, he got away relatively lightly,' says Toon Claes. 'It was fortunate for Remco that he didn't land on a stone or rock. He probably continued to roll, a bit further down.' And, the doctor goes on to add: 'Another positive side to the story was that Remco didn't need to undergo surgery. We were quickly able to predict that the fractures would heal well. Once the injuries had stabilised after a few days *and* the pain was under control, rehabilitation could begin. Indeed, that pain was the biggest initial concern; you shouldn't underestimate the impact of pain.' So far, so good: Remco could begin his rehabilitation, he was prescribed weeks of rest, and he took that rest. 'As long as Remco followed the rules of natural healing, he would heal quickly,' says Dr. Claes.

Only, then it went wrong. 'Remco became too eager. We had warned him not to overdo things, we had clearly impressed upon him what his injuries entailed. I was very familiar with those injuries from personal experience: I once had the exact same fracture after falling off my bike. I too was somewhat careless then, I went and did too much too quickly. The problem with that fracture is that it doesn't actually stop you from being able to cycle to some extent, because the pubic bone fracture is more about small cracks and doesn't really involve any instability. But precisely because you're sitting on the bike, on that saddle, on that injured bone, the injury becomes irritated. Micro-movements occur in the cracks. And that's really not good for the healing of the fracture. To start with, it doesn't feel all that bad, there is some pain during and after cycling, but you think: it will probably pass. In other words, you persist in your stupidity.'

Remco was a bit too eager, he felt good quite quickly and overdid it. The result? He got worse and worse. When he returned for a check-up with Dr Claes, something was immediately apparent on the scans. Oh no, they said in the department: 'That hasn't got better, it's worse.' Remco had no choice but to admit it: his drive had set him back in the healing process. That wasn't planned, of course. But Dr Claes imparts an interesting thought: 'Remco was still very young at the time. And you have to give young people, especially when they have the drive of a strong athlete, the chance to make mistakes. If people – young people – don't get that chance, they have fewer opportunities to develop themselves. There's nothing wrong with making mistakes. Children, for example, have to get that opportunity as well. It's a bad thing if they don't get those opportunities and are overprotected. Such children, such young people often live in a way that holds something back; they are less daring, and they will probably approach the world less assuredly and with less of an open mind. *Never a failure, always a lesson.*'

People learn by their mistakes. Life involves falling and getting up, winning and losing. Remco quickly got that message as well. After he – with his hard-headed approach – had done too much too soon after his serious crash, he took the advice of Dr. Claes, his team, and his entourage to heart. He introduced rest periods, did what others told him, followed their recommendations. That's growing up, that's life.

'The road back to full recovery took months,' says Dr. Claes. 'It was a valuable lesson. Remco had the ability, the openness, and the humility to admit that he had made mistakes. He does that wonderfully well, Remco. Look, there are people who never learn. And there are people who always learn. Remco is someone who always learns. Let me give another example: just compare the way in which Remco rode down a mountain at the beginning of his career to the way he does that now. In Lombardy, at the time of the accident, Remco was very young. Vincenzo Nibali rode the fastest descent of all time in the breakaway, the cycling equivalent of Formula 1, racing at the cutting edge. Nibali also knew the course inside out. He was a highly skilled downhill rider, knew the road like the back of his hand, and he had years of experience. In 2020, Remco was a young lad with no knowledge of the course and only limited experience in descending. A young lad with the bravado to navigate every bend a bit too aggressively and who took risks to do so. Of course, that risk was consistent with the true spirit of a rider looking to succeed. Remco learned from that fall, and he discussed it with the people around him.

And what effect has it had? Remco has become a downhill rider of the highest order.'

In the 2024 Tour of the Basque Country, Remco fell heavily again. A repetition of the fear, the treatment after the fall, the transport, the stabilisation of the broken collarbone, the rehabilitation, the road to recovery. A repetition of the pain. A repetition of the terrible impact on the body. Can we actually imagine – you and I, dear reader – what that impact is like? Do we know what the pain is like for a rider? 'It can only be understood if you crashed once yourself. It can only be understood if you yourself have had the same experience,' says Dr. Claes. 'First, there is the mental aspect: pain is not pleasant, It affects your mind, pain does something to a person. And then there is the physical aspect: minor fractures are never just minor fractures. Not only are they accompanied by pure pain – it simply hurts a lot – but also by the loss of proteins, many sleepless nights, tossing and turning in bed, and a lot of underestimated discomfort.' Non-cyclists cannot imagine the pain of that suffering...

When Remco, on arrival at the hospital, saw his family, the doctors, and his team leaders, he had said 'Sorry' – you just read that from Patrick Lefevere. Doctor Toon Claes ponders for a moment and then says: 'Remco realised himself that he'd gone too far. He meant, "Sorry that I let you down, sorry that I let myself down." Remco will have been thinking – All those people had expected so much from him. All those people now had to upend part of their lives, they had to go to Herentals, they had to support him in his rehabilitation. That realisation probably sank in for Remco there and then.'

In the course of his exceptionally accomplished career, Doctor Toon Claes has come into contact with many top athletes in the sporting world. What characterises those men and women? 'First and foremost, all of them, without exception, have talent. In the absence of talent, they wouldn't make it. At the same time, they are incredibly driven, they know what needs to be done. But then again they're not the only people who are driven, that's true. But those elite performers take it a step further. They can sink their claws into something and then say: this is mine and no one else is going to have it. Elite performers are willing to give everything for it.' But there is yet more, the doctor goes on to say: 'Elite performers also possess an exceptional form of intelligence. And – for sure: they have a pronounced gift for leadership. The presence of a strong team and a solid support system around them, and that this team functions well, is primarily down to them personally. If they want their mechanics, physios, masseurs, doctors, and teammates to dedicate themselves fully, they must be perfectly motivated and guided.' Elite performers are special people, says Doctor Claes. 'All of them have those very specific, rare qualities consolidated in one person. In the world of cycling, Rik Van Looy, back in the 1950s and 1960s, was the first rider to display such leadership, to be a true champion who gathered an entire team around him, motivated it, and got it to work for him – and that team believed in him. In 2024, Remco is also one such person. And he's still growing in that role.'

And, concludes Toon Claes: 'Elite performers are also nice people. They are sympathetic people, grateful people. In their greatness, they are also completely ordinary. After the fall in Lombardy, Remco stayed in the hospital in Herentals for a long time. When he was finally discharged, he brought chocolates for the entire department. He didn't have to do that. But Remco still did.'

The 2021 Giro d'Italia – held in May, between Turin and Milan – marked Remco's comeback after the misery of 2020, which had been so dramatic since that fateful day in mid-August. Exactly 266 days after the fall, he was back. Remco's comeback evoked a lot of excitement in the world of cycling and beyond. For example, the camera crews from VTM, the Flemish commercial channel, followed Remco every step he took. Upon his return, Remco was already extremely ambitious: he was convinced that he could start the Giro with the idea – as he explained in the documentary broadcast on the network – of being race-ready, 'without saying "I want to win". I just want to be ready,' Remco said in all seriousness. Signs of tension were noticeable on his face, it seemed as though Remco had put pressure on himself to be 'good'. 'We've succeeded in that, in other words, I've been working like a maniac to that end,' he said.

Remco performed well in the early stages of the Giro. He didn't win a stage, but his form seemed to be on track. Still, the foundation, after all the misery and wearing himself to a frazzle, was too narrow to really perform. It wasn't that Remco was bad, but in the seventeenth stage – a mountain stage over 193 kilometres from Canazei to Sega di Ala, won by the Irishman Daniel Martin – it was over: Remco quit the Giro d'Italia. That was no disgrace, of course. Remco could now continue to strengthen his foundation. And it wasn't all that long before he started delivering results again. The Baloise Belgium Tour, i.e. the Tour of Belgium, began in Beveren on 9 June. After 175.3 kilometres, through the Flemish Ardennes, Remco finished second in the town of Maarkedal. The next day, he won the time trial in Knokke – it was the place where his teammate Yves Lampaert came up with a nickname for Remco, about which you can read more later. On 13 June, Remco won the overall classification in the Tour of Belgium. He wasn't stopping there. He finished third in the Belgian Road Championship (behind Wout van Aert and Edward Theuns) and second in the time trial (behind Yves Lampaert). Remco was also allowed to go to the (postponed due to coronavirus) Olympic Games in Tokyo. He came ninth in the time trial, with Primož Roglič taking the gold. During the road race, he conserved his energy, launched a bold attack on the Mikuni Pass, but didn't play a significant role thereafter – Richard Carapaz became the Olympic champion, while Wout van Aert brought the silver medal back to Belgium.

Remco was slowly returning to a positive flow; class will tell in the end. That the comeback had been a bit hit-and-miss up to that point didn't particularly matter. Remco started winning again: in the Tour of Denmark, he was victorious in two stages and took the overall victory (plus, of course, the young rider classification!). In the Druivenkoers, near Overijse and not at all far from his own village, Remco performed as usual: he broke away from the group, rode alone at the front, and completed a 60-kilometre solo. His lead: 40 seconds. A few days later, again not a million miles from Schepdaal, the Brussels Cycling Classic was held – the former Paris-Brussels. The race had been given a healthy dose of the Flemish Ardennes thanks to the redrawing of the route. The iconic Muur van Geraardsbergen, or Wall of Geraadsbergen, was included twice in the route on Saturday, 28 August 2021, in the city of (delicious) custard tarts and Manneke Pis statue (the only real one, it's whispered loudly in Geraardsbergen), and the cobblestones of the Vesten, before the riders took the right turn on their way to the Chapel at the top of the Wall – in short, a course that called for controlled racing. That's what the top riders who were present did, they controlled the race. First it was Victor Campenaerts and Remco, then Philippe Gilbert joined, until seven strong riders were left: Remco, Victor and Philippe and Aimé De Gendt, Tosh Van der Sande, Marc Hirschi, and Brandon McNulty. It appeared that the leading group would be instrumental in deciding the winner, but suddenly something peculiar happened: twenty kilometres from the finish, most of the riders followed a motorcyclist to the right, and that was the wrong way – off the course. In an interview afterwards, Remco said, 'I thought: it should be to the left here'. 'I was surprised that they turned right. It's odd that this can still happen, after all, we all have a computer on our bikes,' he said in the flash interview. Being a local rider, Remco knew the course, he knew they still had a cobbled section to go, and that was distinctly not on the right. Remco and Aimé De Gendt took the correct turn and immediately gained a decent lead. 11 kilometres from the finish, Remco made his move. On this occasion, he won with a 20-second lead – after his second solo in three days. Once again, Remco was the rider he had always been. And he rounded off the year 2021 with medals: a silver in the road race and a bronze in the time trial at the European Championships, and a bronze in the World Championship time trial – in his home country.

2022 was a year to remember.

That Remco won the Tour of the Algarve again was almost a mere formality. He also won in Valencia, once again on the Iberian Peninsula. All things considered though, that was small beer compared to what happened on Sunday, 24 April. On that day, the Liège-Bastogne-Liège was held over a distance of 257.1 kilometres. After 6 hours, 12 minutes, and 38 seconds, the winner crossed the line, having a 48-second lead over second place, Quinten Hermans, and third place, Wout van Aert. The winner, that was Remco. Still only 22 years old, the young man had won his first Monument. The way it happened was impressive. Again, it was a solo effort, this time of 30 kilometres. This edition of Liège-Bastogne-Liège was overshadowed by a severe crash: Julian Alaphilippe, Remco's French teammate and reigning world champion, had set his sights on the classic. But a horrific impact put an end to his aspirations – was this not the beginning of a weakened Julian in the years that followed?

Remco felt good, there in the Ardennes sunshine. They were riding on La Redoute, with 29 kilometres still to go. And that's when he went, from behind the back of his teammate who was leading the extended group. Remco's rear wheel pulled away, it was a powerful attack, and all the alarm bells rang for the men behind him. He kept going, Neilson Powless tried to follow, as did Dylan Teuns and Jakob Fuglsang – in vain though, he was gone. The peloton pulled itself together, nothing helped. Racing on still, but riders were dropping off from the lead group, their efforts having been for nought. Keeping it up for yet another 26 kilometres – it had now turned into a race of one against all. With only 2.7 kilometres to go. Remco looked at the cameraman riding alongside him on the motorbike, flashed his cheeky grin, and stuck his fist in the air. Downhill now to the city of Liège. A quick thank you through his earpiece to the team, shaking his head in disbelief, yet it was true: Remco had won Liège-Bastogne-Liège. 'Today was the best day of my career,' he said afterwards. 'It's really fantastic. After that difficult period since the crash, I feel like I'm back at my peak level. I felt good the whole day. I couldn't be happier and I'm proud of the team. What a day on which to finish off the classics season.'

After that, Remco just kept on going: he won three stages in the Tour of Norway (and the overall classification and the young rider classification – what did you expect?), and by now it was the end of May. On the last day of the month, it was the traditional kermis fête in Gullegem, in the heart of West Flanders, a place that breathes cycling and is home to Patrick Lefevere's team. It was time for the 73rd edition of Gullegem Koerse, 'the most famous kermis race in the country' as the organisers themselves like to describe it. They are proud, there in the village. 'After the first edition in 1945, Gullegem was captivated by the sport of cycling: a big crowd, the group of famous riders, and the competitive spirit were the making of the fame that Gullegem Koerse acquired. Remco attacked in West Flanders and won, after – surprise, surprise! – a solo. His lead? 1 minute and 22 seconds.

Remco won the time trial in the Tour of Switzerland, and he won the Belgian time trial championship. Remco won the Clásica San Sebastián, after yet another powerful solo. The summer of 2022 gradually progressed into August, and in the meantime, Jonas Vingegaard had won the Tour de France, with a 2'43" lead over Tadej Pogačar and 7'22" ahead of Geraint Thomas. Remco was preparing for the Tour of Spain, the Vuelta. 'Remco had gone there with the idea of aiming for a top 10 finish, possibly even top 5. That was his ambition,' says father Patrick. 'Anything more would have been a bonus.' The Vuelta started on 19 August in Utrecht, the Netherlands an unusual diversion introduced by the organisers. Primož Roglič was the hot favourite, since he'd previously won the Vuelta a España three times and the stage race suited him well. After three stages in the Netherlands, there was now a rest day – after all, the caravan still had to make its way to Spain, where the Vuelta would truly begin. Difficult stages then ensued – hilly and mountainous stages. The 29 August was another rest day. 'The day after that was a time trial in Alicante,' says Patrick. 'That immediately became Remco's first objective. He had reconnoitred the route several times in the winter, he wanted to win that time trial.' And he did. But in the days before that time trial, something was already noticeable: 'In the first week, with all that climbing, Remco had performed well. He had ridden extremely well uphill for the whole of the first week in Spain, so much so that he even wore the leader's jersey,' relates Patrick. 'I was sitting with Patrick Lefevere at the time, and we were wondering how things would pan out from now on. "And now?" we'd said to each other. We decided it was best to take it day by day. It was actually going perfectly; he won a second stage, this being a mountain stage. Remco had just one more bad moment, which came two days after a stupid fall. He lost some time then, but he remained on track to win the Tour of Spain. Whether there might have been a battle with Roglič to the very end, we'll never know. Primož had to abandon the Vuelta after coming off,' Patrick tells. In any case: Remco won his first Grand Tour. He had a 2'02" lead on Enric Mas and 4'57" on Juan Ayuso.

As stated: 2022 was a year to remember. Remco had won both a Monument and a Grand Tour. With the world championship still to come.

'That was in Australia,' says Patrick Evenepoel. 'On account of the time difference, we were already up and ready for the TV from 4 a.m. on Sunday, 25 September. By then, they'd already started broadcasting the road race live.' A dense crowd had gathered In Café In de Rustberg after Remco's victory — 'If they'd counted the people then, they would have reached several thousand,' says Guy. He is the owner of the café and represents the fourth generation behind the bar. They started here in 1906 – that was my great-grandfather,' he says. 'Next door, there was also a cooperage where he made barrels, casks, and tubs. The workshop for it stood over there but it's gone now. Demolished,' says Guy. His grandfather and father succeeded his great-grandfather, and now Guy has been the café owner for 40 years. Here, a filter coffee with a proper spoon on the saucer and a biscuit costs only €2.50, and the slate club box is still hanging on the wall — but we don't use it any more, those days are gone. Ever since Remco began his cycling career and rode his first races, the café has been the supporter's hub for the local boy. Hanging on the walls are jerseys that bear witness to Remco's meteoric rise, alongside photos of the triumphant local hero in the Grand Tours – it resembles the modest beginnings of a small museum collection. Outside, on the side wall of the façade, a mural has been painted: Remco in large, the date at the bottom proves that they've been with him from the very beginning: '2018', no less. At the front, in the large car park, there's a kind of sculpture – a stylised cyclist, and Remco's results are regularly updated on the artwork, says Guy. And goes on to say: 'People now come from all over to have a look and have a drink here. Some come here after riding up the hill but then have to stop, simply because they can't go any further. It's called the Rustberg, or Mountain Rest, for a reason. Others start here on the R.EV route, a lovely ride along signposted roads.' Hang on, says Guy: 'I'll just fetch my iPad. Then you can see the photos that show how many people were here on that day in September 2022. Just a second, I'll be right back.' Guy was right, as proven by the pictures he has saved: there was a huge crowd. 'Want another coffee?' he enquires. Two men ride up on a bike – electric. They speak English, with a distinct American accent, and sit down at a table in the full sun, next to three women in cycling apparel – a world champion, a green jersey wearer, and a proud wearer of the polka dot jersey. A week earlier, on Sunday, 18 September, something funny had happened at the World Championship time trial: Remco had come in third. There was nothing wrong with that per se, he had earned another medal. But when he rolled over the finish line, he was surprised about the winner. That had been Noor Tobias Foss. A respectable time trial rider, but the favourite? No, not at all. Remco was shocked. He'd taken off his helmet and removed his earpiece. Then he took a towel and rubbed it over his head, drank from a bottle of water, and said: 'Huh? Foss?' He raised his eyebrows and drank again – Foss? Yeah, that was a surprise.

The road race covered 266.9 kilometres. The critical factor on the course: Mount Pleasant. No, it wasn't pleasant for Remco's competitors. With two laps to go before the end of the race, he was away, launching into an extraordinary performance. Only Alexey Lutsenko, the hard charger from Kazakhstan, made attempts to follow, but he knew it was a lost cause. He held on for a little longer, until the inevitable happened and he saw Remco ride away, with 25 kilometres still to go. Remco became world champion, having secured the rainbow jersey after 6 hours, 16 minutes, and 8 seconds. 2 minutes and 22 seconds later, a sprint took place for the other two places on the podium. Take a moment, dear reader, and reflect once more on the lead: two minutes and twenty-one seconds! And take another moment to check the names of the riders in that sprinting pack — they read like an entry from the encyclopaedia of the best riders of the 21st century: Christophe Laporte (in 2nd), Michael Matthews (in 3rd), Wout van Aert, Matteo Trentin, Alexander Kristoff, Peter Sagan (jawel! And then! In 7th!), Alberto Bettiol, Ethan Hayter, Mattias Skjelmose, Ivan Garcia, Jan Tratnik, Lorenzo Rota, Ben Tulett, Mikkel Honoré, Rasmus Tiller, Mauro Schmid, Neilson Powless, Tadej Pogačar (in 19th!), Stefan Küng, Kévin Geniets, Romain Bardet, Attila Valter, Alexey Lutsenko, Bauke Mollema, Benoît Cosnefroy, Dylan van Baarle, Pascal Eenkhoorn – all sprinting for honour, for their country, and for themselves, at 2'21" behind.

Remco was thrilled after earning his title. In his first comments, he called it 'a title that couldn't be compared to the junior ones.' He spoke off the cuff in English for the UCI microphone: 'I cannot compare this with the juniors. It's a lot more hours of racing and it's much, much harder.' And – in a colossal understatement: 'I wanted to go it alone. I had the legs today. You cannot afford to lose any time on this circuit. The last lap was really tough, my legs were exploding. But I knew it was nearly over. The team car was telling me that my lead was extending.' Then Remco paid compliment to the Belgian team: 'We raced like a real team.'

At the end of the interview, Remco made a bold statement: 'I've won everything I could. I don't think I'll ever have a better season. Well: he had won a classic – a Monument – and won both a Grand Tour and the World Championship. That was extremely impressive, he'd done what very few riders before him had done: Alfredo Binda in 1927, Eddy Merckx in 1971, and Bernard Hinault in 1980 (Tadej Pogačar will do the same in 2024). Of course, Remco couldn't know at the time what the magical summer of 2024 was yet to bring.

The UCI reporter had one more question: 'Are you going to have a little party tonight?' Remco laughed: 'Yeah! A big one! I'm not gonna see my bed, I guess!' On the other side of the world, that party was already in full swing. Supporters danced and sang, cheered and celebrated. Mother Agna, father Patrick, beloved Oumi were a bundle of emotions; they were proud, happy, thankful. There were tears and laughter, Remco had achieved all this and they had all experienced it up close, the victories, the ascent to where he was now, to where they were now, they had explored the deep lows together and then overcome them together. Agna, Patrick, and Oumi were relieved that it had all worked out, they were astounded by the degree of success. Tuesday would come around before long. They just had to wait another two days. Then they would be able to wrap their arms around Remco.

On 7 October 2022, a top year was transformed into a magnificent champagne year. Remco, aged 22, and Oumi Rayane, also 22, got married in the town hall of Dilbeek, the small town in Brabant to which Schepdaal belongs. Remco arrived driving a white, classic car – a convertible MGB sportscar, no less. It was a bright, sunny day, perfect for having the top down. Remco was smiling at the wheel, in his grey suit – or was it perhaps more green? Sitting next to him was Oumi, in a white bridal dress. She had been Remco's girlfriend from a young age, his companion on the road, his partner. In the presence of joyful parents and family, their marriage was a beautiful union of two cultures that had come together: the boy, a native of Brussels, and the girl with Moroccan roots.

Oumi is 25 years old in 2024 and, as previously mentioned, has Moroccan roots, on both her father's and mother's sides. Her father was born in Belgium, her mother grew up in Marrakesh. In 1997, her father went on holiday to Morocco, where he fell in love with a ravishing young woman – and you know how it goes, dear reader, the young woman became his wife. They established their life together in Lennik, in a charming house among the fields of Brussels' rural outskirts. Oumi was the first child born to the family, to be followed by three brothers. The Rayane family was doing well. Her father was the manager of a taxi firm in Brussels, her mother took care of the children at home. Oumi played in the large garden, enjoying the outdoor life – the young girl was an active child, always busy, always energetic, constantly tending to the chickens and running riot with the kids in the neighbourhood. She enjoyed the village, the greenery, and the space. The four children went to school in Lennik, first to the primary school, later to the secondary school.

But in 2016, the Rayane family relocated to a bigger house. As a result, they ended up in the village next to Lennik: that village being Schepdaal. Just a few months earlier, another family had also moved to Schepdaal, to a house on the same street, but 200 metres further along. That family, was the Evenepoel family. Oumi continued going to school in Lennik, where she felt at home. And the new boy next door (almost) from Schepdaal also went to that school. When that boy – who went by the name of Remco – saw the girl in the playground, it was love at first sight. Remco deployed all his charms in the battle, but Oumi preferred to concentrate on her studies. But before long, the two young people realised that they got on really well together. They really wanted to be more than just friends. Something was growing between them, slowly but surely, and why should they try to resist it? Life seemed so great when they were together, just the two of them. On top of that, luck smiled even more on Oumi and her family around that time – after three little brothers – she got a little sister, Amira. In short, things were perfect around those weeks. Oumi had not only become a big sister, she was not only the friend and neighbour of the young lad who went to her school and lived in the same street as her. Oumi and Remco were now also girlfriend and boy-friend. Oumi laughs fondly: 'We started arranging to do our homework together after school, or getting on the bus to the centre of Brussels to wander around,' she recounts. And she adds: 'Meanwhile, Remco was discovering more and more that he had a passion for cycling.'

Remco became Remco, the cyclist you know and admire, the person you're reading about in this book. Oumi went to study Applied Economic Sciences at VUB, the Vrije Universiteit Brussel. 'Remco's cycling career is number 1, that remains the absolute priority. I want it to continue running smoothly,' says Oumi. 'But I also want to make the most of my abilities, which is why, alongside racing, I'm pursuing higher education. We are both really keen for me to get my university degree.' In the meantime, they are living their life to the full – *full gas*. 'That's true,' says Oumi. 'But we try to alternate that life at *full gas* with *full rest* and moments of relaxation. We can really enjoy a Sunday of doing nothing with a big breakfast, a true morning of refined pleasure, a *take-it-easy morning*.' Such a pleasant Sunday of doing nothing often doesn't actually fall on an actual Sunday. The reason for that is simple: 'Our Sunday is usually in the middle of the week,' says Oumi, 'because Sundays usually involve racing.' And while Remco is off to training camps and competitions, Oumi focuses on her studies and also takes care of household matters. 'Then, when Remco gets home, there is full rest.' Yes, every now and then there are posts on social media about their activities; after all Oumi and Remco are young and they are the children of their time. There is then occasionally talk of so-called *wife duties*: 'All the usual and obvious household tasks,' says Oumi. But there is (much) more than that: 'That also means ensuring balanced meals as per the nutrition plans. Or keeping an eye on administrative matters, looking after things so that Remco doesn't have to be overburdened with them during the season.' And – even more and just as important (or perhaps even more important): staying motivated, continuing to analyse what is going well and what could be better, and keeping both feet on the ground. Oumi ponders for a moment and then continues: 'Sometimes there are moments when

Remco gets nervous. Then I can have a calming effect. And I also tell him if something bothers me or if he is, in my opinion, doing something wrong. That helps him to maintain his focus at those moments when it's necessary.'

This is how Remco and Oumi have grown together in their relationship, in their love for each other. They've learnt to know each other better and better, to know their individual selves better, with and through each other: 'Remco has awakened my interest in the world of cycling and other sports. I've learned to be more independent by living with him. I'm often on my own when Remco is away.' Oumi laughs softly: 'Formerly, at home with my parents, I was a pampered little princess. And Remco? Now Remco has acquired three brothers and a sister. He has a strong connection to them. They have a lot of fun together, lovely family fun.' Later – at the end of this book – you'll get a glimpse of this small, personal happiness of a young couple, together on an outing after one of Remco's incredible achievements. It will be during a moment of family togetherness in the middle of the night, somewhere in a beautiful city.

Oumi experienced the story of ups and downs from the front row – Lombardy was a sledgehammer blow. Things happened on 15 August 2020 that will be etched in someone's memory forever. Things happened on that day that first of all break a person and then – eventually – make them stronger, once the pieces have been put back together. People – young people – grow up quickly in such circumstances. 'As a partner, you are also emotionally broken by such serious crashes and injuries,' says Oumi. 'Then your job is to switch off the negativity as quickly as possible and bring out only positive vibes, so that Remco regains confidence in a successful recovery process. When Remco was lying in a hospital bed at home in 2020, I was in the middle of an exam period. I put the exams to the side at the time so I could be there for Remco as much as possible.' Allow these words to sink in for a moment, dear reader: 'Remco was unable to walk on his own then, nor could he eat unassisted. Or go to the toilet.' And so, Oumi spent long days at Remco's and his parents' home – to be with him.

Oumi, 25 years old, a young woman who is conscious of her values and principles, and who herself says: 'I will respect those to my dying day. Never will I do anything that goes against my principles. I'll go through the fire for my friends and family. I understand that I've been given many privileges by my parents. I often think of others and feel concerned for those who are less fortunate. That's why I get involved in social projects.'

Oumi, 25 years old, a young woman with a heart of gold – caring for the people around her.
Oumi and Remco, grew up together, developed together from teenagers into young adults.
Their engagement and marriage have introduced a lot of stability into their lives together, Oumi says. And later, Remco will say the same.
Oumi concludes: 'Our marriage, it anchors us and it's a *blessing*, enabling us to do things in our own way and let off steam together after intense periods in cycling and my studies.'

Then along came 2023.
Remco won Liège-Bastogne-Liège on 23 April of that year.
That was for the second year in a row.
He had a 1'06" lead over Tom Pidcock – no laggard himself.
On 6 May, the 106th Giro d'Italia started in Fossacesia.
Remco won the first stage.
It was a time trial to Ortona, distance: just under 20 kilometres.
Remco immediately donned the pink leader's jersey.
The fifth stage went from Atripalda to Salerno.
That day, 10 May, it rained hard.
Remco fell twice.
The pink leader's jersey was handed over to the Norwegian, Andres Leknessund.
The ninth stage was ridden on 14 May.

It was a time trial from Savigno sul Rubicone to Cesena.

The distance: 35 kilometres.

Remco won the time trial.

Then there was a rest day.

And Remco departed from the Giro.

He'd been struck down by coronavirus.

Rest restored him to health and fitness.

On 11 August, the World Time Trial Championship for elite riders was held in Stirling, Scotland. The course was 47.8 kilometres in length.

Remco won and became world champion.

He'd won a classic and he'd become world champion

Not bad going.

Remco could relax.

And then prepare himself for a new year.

He could get himself ready for 2024.

Remco would then be 24 years old.

Still only 24 years old.

18

'ON THE
WAY BACK IN
THE CAR, NOT A
WORD WAS SAID.
THE TEARS WERE
RUNNING DOWN
OUR CHEEKS.'

Critérium du Dauphiné.
There is a fascination about this race. There are things about this stage race that give it something extra.

First of all, there's the name, it sounds simply wonderful. The course was named after the newspaper – *Le Dauphiné Libéré* – which after the Second World War had decided in 1947 to organise a stage race in the south of France. *Le Dauphiné Libéré* is a regional newspaper, situated in de Hautes-Alpes, Ardèche, Drôme, Vaucluse. That heavenly holiday region of sun and good food, quaint alleyways in wonderfully picturesque villages, with a Bar Tabac in the square where that other (sports) newspaper, *L'Équipe*, lies on the table, against a background of plain trees and snuffling dogs looking to bask in the first heat of the year.

The Dauphiné is a great race, with great winners: Jacques Anquetil, Raymond Poulidor, Luis Ocaña, Bernard Thévenet, Eddy Merckx, Michel Pollentier, Bernard Hinault, Alejandro Valverde, Chris Froome. Primož Roglič, Jonas Vingegaard – you know their names.

But the Dauphiné is more than a great name with great winners. It is also the race of hope and expectation. It is the race where not everything has to be perfect yet, but going in that direction. The riders want to check their readiness for when the Tour de France comes around at the end of June. Secretly, they are already hoping for a sweet victory here in the Dauphiné, for that would bode well. They are getting a head start on the great things that will follow – it's like the first barbecue on the first summer's day, even before summer has really started, it's like the taste of surprisingly delicious sausages, with an unexpectedly good glass of rosé, it's like the holiday that is about to truly begin. A victory in the Dauphiné is one of those moments: how great everything is, and soon there will be even more of that to come.

In 2024, Remco took part in the Critérium du Dauphiné for the first time. He set off for the stage race with question marks in his mind. That was

hardly surprising: Remco had spent the entire month of May in rehabilitation after an immensely serious crash in the Tour of the Basque
Country. On Thursday, 4 April, the fourth stage was raced in the north
of Spain in the Vuelta Ciclista al País Vasco, or something unpronounce-
able in Basque: that day was yet another tricky stage – the stages in the
Basque Country are always challenging, always tough, always over hills
and mountains, never really flat, always undulating. And, on top of all
that, it's often awful weather. The fourth stage encompassed 157.5 kilometres from Etxarri to Aranatz. If you search for the results of the stage
on the internet, you'll discover that Louis Meintjes of Intermarché-
Wanty was the winner. But you'll notice as well that very little attention
is paid to the South African's victory. The greatest victory in Meintjes'
career was secondary. Because after more than 118 kilometres, in the
descent from the second climb of the day, the Olaeta, fate struck.

'We were sat here in the shop watching the live broadcast on television
with friends,' says Patrick Evenepoel. We saw that on a peculiar bend
between the trees riders were coming off there. At first sight, we thought
that Remco had managed to avoid it. But when they showed the replay,
we saw him lying among the trees.' Patrick and his mates held their
breath – 'It can't be, can it?!' For a moment nothing was said, then they
looked back at the screen, and thought: phew! Because, says Patrick: 'We
saw Remco on his feet, moving around. We thought he must be OK.' But
the footage revealed how Remco – in his Belgian champion's jersey –
was gripping his shoulder and being escorted to his team's support car.
A bit further off, between the trees, the carnage was severe: Primož
Roglič was lying in a concrete drainage ditch – after long, anxious minutes, he indicated with a thumbs-up that he was (more or less) OK. But
Jonas Vingegaard, Jay Vine, Steff Cras, Sean Quinn weren't so lucky.
Stretchers and ambulances were called for, the race was halted, but then
restarted with the leaders allowed – away from the peloton – to still
compete for the stage victory.

'I immediately received a message from Remco,' says Patrick 'He was en route to the hospital; he said his shoulder was hurting. He texted that it wasn't serious and that we would stay in touch.' That was reassuring. Leastwise, so it appeared. But, says Patrick: 'Straight away it gave me a kind of déjàvu feeling. I thought immediately about what had happened in the 2020 Tour of Lombardy. I thought immediately of the journey Remco had undergone in the preceding months. All those preparations, all those stages, all those sacrifices. I thought immediately of him, that young guy, and of Oumi, his young girlfriend.' The team around Remco got in touch with Toon Claes, the doctor, photos of the shoulder were discussed. 'We're going to operate on Saturday,' was the decision.

The operation went perfectly, it's true. But, says Patrick: 'Then the mental battle starts all over again.' It's the battle to clear your mind, spending hours in rehabilitation, pulling yourself back together, picking yourself up again. It became, in short, a special kind of fight again: the head had to prepare the legs, the body, and the shoulder for great performances again. Or, as Patrick describes it: 'Coming back? No doubt that was physically possible. But coming back stronger? Giving it your all mentally? That's a whole different ball game. But anyone who wants to get to the top has to be able to do that, must do it. Whoever is not able to come back mentally stronger will be left behind.'

And Remco came back, stronger than ever, as you know.

Patrick Evenepoel revisits the events he briefly mentioned in the first chapter of this book. He fondly refers again to two incidents that occurred when Remco was still the young footballer. Patrick puts it like this: 'These were two moments when we felt that Remco was going to achieve something in life, and he was still just a child.'

This was the first moment: Remco excelled as a footballer. When he was eleven, he had the opportunity of going to Racing Genk – 'We got a fantastic reception there,' says Patrick – or he could go to PSV Eindhoven

– 'There too we got a fantastic reception.' Remco opted for the most difficult path, the one to the Netherlands, to PSV. It meant hours in the car to get to training sessions and matches. 'Until after a year of travelling back and forth, Remco went to the club's management and said he didn't want to do it any more,' continues Patrick. Remco had made a decision: he wanted to go to a host family. Now, more than 10 years later, Patrick has this to say: 'Our kid was about to turn 12, and then he decided on his own to go and live with a host family. Because it was better for his career, for his peace of mind. That was hard for us, for Agna and me as parents. The first time we dropped him off in Eindhoven, we didn't say a word in the car on the way back. The tears were running down our cheeks.' Patrick pauses momentarily, engrossed in thinking about that car journey, and then says: 'You have only one child.' They had glanced back for a moment, Patrick and Agna, as they drove out of the street, and had seen Remco standing there. He had waved briefly and turned around: 'He was gone. Remco didn't make a big thing of it.'

Then there was also that second moment. Remco had ended up on the bench at Anderlecht. It must have been some time in November or December. A few weeks later, in January, he would be 17 years old. Remco was fed up with the situation and a meeting with the club's staff was arranged. Those present were the manager, Herman Van Holsbeeck, the head of the youth department, Jean Kindermans, father Patrick and Remco himself. The tone of the conversation was that Anderlecht couldn't be more satisfied with Remco's mentality. But: they wanted to qualify for the Youth League with Anderlecht, against teams of the calibre of FC Barcelona and such. And, the people in charge said: 'For that, we need bears, strong players with height and weight. Remco didn't have that stature, being neither heavy or tall – he wasn't a bear. Remco didn't get this reasoning. But the management reassured him: in the New Year he could be back on the team. Remco could even become captain again – there was actually no problem, according to Anderlecht. But then this happened, recounts Patrick: 'Remco stood up and said: "I won't come any more." Really and truly: he got up and I was just sitting there. He shook hands with the big bosses and walked out of the meeting.'

Four months later, in April 2017, Remco Evenepoel was no longer a footballer. He had become a cyclist. That was no whim. It was an indication of Remco's immense self-confidence: he thinks long and hard about the advantages and disadvantages, takes his time to make a decision, but once his mind is made up, he does not waver. Or in other words: Remco has a strong head on his shoulders and he doesn't just do things on impulse.

Remco is always mentally prepared for the things that are about to happen. And that was the case again in the aftermath of the crash in the Basque Country. It was three weeks before he could get back on a bike, and after that, he had to spend hours and hours and hours rebuilding the foundation. Remco wanted to be ready for his first Tour de France – that was what his head had ordered him to do, now he just needed to find the legs for it. In the early days after the crash, he was forging plans with doctors and physiotherapists.

But before the Tour, first came the Critérium du Dauphiné. When the race started on 2 June 2024 in Saint-Pourçain-sur-Sioule with a stage of 172.5 kilometres – won by Mads Pedersen – Remco was still experiencing some doubts: how would his shoulder hold up? Plus: Remco was not yet at his ideal weight; he could still lose one or two kilos and then he would be razor-sharp. With the proper training, the right nutritional advice, and his own iron will, that would also be achievable towards the start of the Tour a few weeks later.

On 5 June, there was an individual time trial between Saint-Germain-Laval and Neulise over a distance of 34.4 kilometres. Remco had thoroughly prepared for it, together with team leader Klaas Lodewyck. The last 10 kilometres of a rather scenic course, which followed a route through typical French villages, were surveyed twice. Since his days as a junior, Remco has maintained a fixed routine in preparation for a time trial: breakfast, warm-up, surveying the course by car or bike, and warming up again on the rollers, up until 10 minutes before he has to get on the starting podium – it's a question of warming up the engine. There, on the rollers, a rider knows whether it will feel right later in real. There, on the rollers, Remco knows how things stand.

Remco rode the second part of the time trial to Neulise cautiously. Patrick had already noticed that when he saw the footage of his son on the live TV stream. The analysis that Jacky Durand – ex-cyclist and the 1992 winner of the Tour of Flanders – provided after the finish in *Les Rois de la Pédale* on Eurosport validated what Patrick was thinking: Durand had noticed that Remco took the technical section of the course differently through the bends compared to someone like Primož Roglič. The Slovenian took risks, coming into every bend with one hand off the handlebars. Remco was still steering as normal for the bend. In the bends, Remco lost two seconds to that other young rider who was riding assertively: Joshua Tarling. But after each bend, Remco pulled himself together, went full gas, and pulled ahead. He won the time trial with a 17-second lead on Tarling and 39 seconds on Roglič.

Remco was happy; he had a good feeling. In the evening, while on the massage table with physiotherapist David Geeroms, he messaged his family accordingly. With the hectic nature of the race, that was all he could manage: the people Remco cares about had to accept that. Even in an organisation like the Critérium du Dauphiné, it's not simple to just phone through to Schepdaal.

But the foundation that Remco had built up over the past few weeks was still on the fragile side. He lost time in the subsequent stages. Not by very much, but enough. In the end, after eight days of riding, that resulted in placing seventh in the final classification of the Critérium du Dauphiné, 2 minutes and 25 seconds behind the winner, Roglič.

And yet: the signals being given off by Remco were good. No: they were exceptionally good. Team leader Klaas and physiotherapist David noticed it in Remco's vicinity. Patrick, Agna, and Oumi heard it in the conversations and read it in the messages: the legs still had some work to do, but in his mind, Remco was ready for what would be coming.

And that was the Tour.

19

'THE CROISSANTS
AND WHITE BREAD
ROLLS FROM THE
BAKER'S WIFE
NAOMI TASTE EVEN
BETTER NOW.'

It's often said that the Giro d'Italia is harder.

Or that the mountains in the Vuelta a España are higher, crueler.

But the Tour de France is the greatest race.

Why is that? Often, the same riders are at the start, usually the same teams appear, and sometimes it involves the same mountains. And yet: the Tour is greater.

Why is that? Simple, in all probability: for the viewers and supporters, it's a holiday. The Giro, that is still in May, when the mornings are spent in rush hour traffic going to work and the childcare centre. And then gradually, thoughts turn to exams and the stress associated with them – will sons and daughters pass them successfully? And in September, the nights start to draw in, the traffic jams are longer, daughters and sons are moving up to a higher school year after passing their exams more than two months previously. It's then time for the Vuelta, and in Spain, the sun is still shining. But holiday time? No, that feeling is long gone.

At the end of June, the days are long, the croissants and white bread rolls from the baker's wife Naomi taste (even) better than during the rest of the year, at half past ten in the morning it's already time for the first aperitif, the newspapers are writing about the grass at Wimbledon, and soon the sausages will be going on the grill. In short, it's Tour de France time – and that's what makes the Tour so great.

Of course, there's more to it than that. The best riders in the elite peloton are in peak form in June and July; they have been building up to the biggest race of the year. It is during those twenty days that they have to perform, under great pressure and immense attention from the press and the public. That also makes the Tour so special: now you have to make it happen.

In 2024, Belgium had been waiting 48 years for a successor to Lucien Van Impe. In the long, hot summer of 1976, a few months shy of his thirtieth birthday, Lucien made his dream reality: he had won the Tour. He was the best climber of his day – perhaps even the best climber there has ever been. He won the mountain classification six times in the Tour de France; in the Giro, he did that twice. An overall victory in the Tour had been nigh on impossible for Van Impe up until 1976. After all, there was Eddy Merckx (and also, in 1975, Bernard Thévenet). Lucien Van Impe knew that during the Merckx era, it was difficult to win the Tour; no one had to foist any illusions onto the realist from Mere in East Flanders. Until, in 1976, he set Belgium on fire: on 18 July of that year, he became the overall winner, the greatest triumph of his rich and long career – he didn't stop until he was in his 41st year.

Lucien Van Impe was ahead of his time: in the 1970s he was the first rider that exercised focus. In his case on the Tour de France – year on year his goal was the stage race. It's true that he also rode classics. For example, he finished sixth in Liège-Bastogne-Liège, thirteenth in the Tour of Flanders, and ninth in the Flèche Wallonne, and in 1975 he finished ninth at the World Championships. But as soon as the Tour de Romandie was approaching – sometime in early May – Lucien was at his best. He then went on to win mountain stages, time trials, and mountain jerseys in the characteristic preparatory races for the Tour at the time: the Midi Libre, the Tour de l'Aude, the Dauphiné Libéré, and the Tour of Switzerland. Lucien's focus was bold. Because if his Tour went badly, then his entire year went badly. In the end, it rarely happened that Lucien messed up a Tour: he started 15 times, never gave up, stood on the podium four times, won nine stages, and was King of the Mountains six times. His worst – or better expressed: his least good result, was 27th place at the end of his career.

Lucien Van Impe spoke about that focus, about his approach, some time ago in his own biography, *Lucien! How I, as the last Belgian, won the Tour*. He puts it like this: 'That remark, that I only rode the Tour de France, was thrown at me hundreds of times. I would like to qualify that. Yes, the Tour got my undivided attention. I cannot deny that. But in the flat preparatory races in the south of France and in Spain, around mid-February, I was always there as well. So I really did start the season early. In 1976, though, and by way of exception, I started somewhat later. Due to my hernia surgery, my preference was to skip the first competitions this time. I didn't want to overexert myself. I hardly ever won in that early stage, it's true, but that didn't matter either. I covered kilometres and decided for myself where and when I would go into the red, where I would drop out, where I wanted to join in with a leading group, and where I would ease off. I didn't have a set programme, drawn up by team managers or team leaders. I decided everything for myself, drew up my own schedules, and made it simple for myself: I just rode everything. I never went all out, it was all training. I also did my work for my teammates, who were keen to win so early in the year. I thought that was good: it was enjoyable for morale. After the races in the South, I headed down to what was then still known as the Omloop Het Volk. This was followed by all the classics. This is what the simple plan that I devised for myself looked like. That's all there was to it.

In the winter, I had put on some 5 to 6 kilograms. Those extra kilos were the result of less training, less racing. I loosened my belt in mid-October and only started training lightly again in the last week of December or the first week of January. I didn't gain weight due to a different, less strict eating pattern. I sometimes indulged during the winter months, but that didn't happen very often. 'The race is won in the winter,' is what my father told me once. I remembered that: I watched my diet, rested a lot, and didn't go out much. I thought those 5 kilograms were OK, they gave me some winter fat, a reserve layer. It was the foundation for a good season. Gradually, I could work towards my competition weight: 59 kilograms was the ideal, perfect for my height at 1.67 metres. I weighed myself twice a day, once in the morning and once in the evening. Upon waking I would check my pulse, 42 to 44 beats per minute being ideal at rest. My pulse told me a lot about my overall condition. I could quickly tell whether I was going to get sick or if I had the flu because then it would increase. That's all there was to it, I just stuck to my plan. I could do that too, I knew my own body down to the minutest fibres. I didn't need any help. I noted my readings and compared them to the previous year's ones. It didn't have to be any more complicated.

In 1976, I did well in the classics. I thought that was a good omen: I would have a brilliant year of racing. After Liège-Bastogne-Liège, I never returned home but travelled on to the Tour de Romandië. That's where I started to build up gradually. In May and early June, the races I preferred to prepare for were approaching: the Tour de l'Aude, the Midi Libre, and the Dauphiné Libéré. Great courses, and with the first real mountains as well. They were my kind of courses: the stages weren't too long but very hard nonetheless. Ideal for loosening me up a bit before the real Tour. I often rode well there and I usually won a stage or gained the mountain classification. I enjoyed it. But then came the stress. After the preparatory races, the fear set in. Now, so close to the Tour, I couldn't afford to get sick or have a fall. I then deliberately rode very few races. My focus on the Tour put immense pressure on me. In the weeks leading up to the 1976 Tour, I became a pain in the neck, a difficult guy. "Just leave Dad alone," Rita would say to our children, Bart and Suzy. "Try not to make too much noise, kids." Rita said that I could gradually start to set off. "The children are fed up with it." I literally started counting down. Now it could really start. I was ready for it.'

Three-and-a-half weeks later, Lucien won the Tour de France.

20

'IT IS AND
WILL REMAIN MY
FIRST TOUR. IT'S
GOING TO BE ONE
GIANT VOYAGE
OF DISCOVERY.'

Remco was preparing himself for his first Tour – that of 2024 – in Isola 2000, a place in the French Alps, in the Provence-Alpes-Côte d'Azur region (in the Alpes-Maritimes department, close to the Italian border). At an average altitude of 2,000 metres, the area is ideal for winter sports, and hence its name, Isola 2000. But it's also a suitable place for cyclists to go for altitude training. Remco went there after the Dauphiné, and Tadej Pogačar was there as well. In itself, it was not surprising that both riders stayed there. 'Top athletes take the same route when building their fitness,' says father Patrick on the subject. 'Their respective preparations don't differ all that much. They know exactly what they have to do and are supported by an entourage that knows what's what. In liaison with Remco, team manager Klaas Lodewyck worked up the plan for such training. What Remco and the other top athletes want is to become even better, even stronger. They want to take it another step higher. Elite athletes have the mindset for that, something I've mentioned a few times already. And of course they also have that powerful engine, which makes enduring it slightly less hard for them.' Patrick puts it another way as well: 'Being at such a training camp is like fun for those top athletes, they can handle it. These are men who enjoy themselves and work hard at the same time.' Patrick made this statement weeks before the big engines withdrew to Isola 2000 for their intense labour. And what he said was spot on, as a quote from Tadej Pogačar in the next paragraph will confirm.

Pogačar was already in top form when he arrived in Isola 2000 on 3 June. Just a few days earlier he'd inscribed his name on the Giro d'Italia: on the podium in Rome on 26 May, Tadej had a 9'56" lead over Colombian Daniel Martinez of BORA-hansgrohe and a 10'24" lead over Welshman Geraint Thomas of INEOS Grenadiers. Followers had agreed in their comments that Pogačar had shown the best version of himself during the three weeks of the Giro. The Slovenian won six stages and essentially left only crumbs for his (distant) competitors. That he was now also preparing for the Tour was remarkable. Tadej's plan was daring. For some time now, top athletes have been opting to focus on a few well-chosen goals; after one goal, they withdraw from competition, go to (altitude) training camps, and prepare for the next goal there, under the guidance of their trainers and nutritionists. Sometimes on their own, sometimes in the company of teammates. Not since Marco Pantani in 1998 had a rider won both the Giro and the Tour de France in one and the same year. And that was precisely the goal Pogačar set for himself in 2024. Daring, thus. But he had every confidence in his own ability – he felt he could perform in the Tour, barely a month after the Giro. On Instagram, he posted images of fun rides and intense sessions with captions like: *'Hard work but great times here at the pre-tour camp.'* Pogačar was looking forward to it. And why shouldn't he? Live wire that he is, he had no issue with losing motivation (or didn't allow it to get to him) nor was anything preying on his mind, everything was going without a hitch – until he had to cut the training camp short by three days due to the death of his grandfather.

For Remco, at the start of the altitude camp in Isola 2000, it was more a case of experimenting, finding his way gradually. The Dauphiné went quite well, as you've already read above. The urge to lay down a remarkable performance in the Tour was without question present. However, some fine-tuning was still needed, the finishing touches, and there were only three weeks left in which to do that. As stated earlier: the legs still had to be conditioned for what the head had already decided on. The sports columns in the most popular newspapers in Remco's home country – *Het Laatste Nieuws* and *Het Nieuwsblad* – were making a big deal of it. In *Het Laatste Nieuws*, the headline read: 'One-and-a-half kilos shed in 2 weeks. That takes character.' The article, spread over two full pages, was published on Wednesday, 26 June 2024. In the introduction to the piece Remco spoke about the conditions in Isola 2000: a lot of rain, low temperatures, and chilly for the time of year. In such weather, Remco picked up a (slight) cold – the exact reason for him calling off his participation in the Belgian road championship a few days before the start of the Tour. When Remco looked back on the Dauphiné, he felt – according to his own assessment – that he was still about 15% short. In the article, Remco mentioned the one-and-a-half kilograms he still aimed (or ought) to lose. In the few days left before the start of the Tour, he also managed to achieve that. 'It should help me perform better in the mountains later on,' he said. In *Het Nieuwsblad* on that same day, it was phrased like this: 'With what I weighed after the Dauphiné, I'd never be able to keep up with the top riders in the Tour. It was hard work but I've managed it.' In that article, Remco also briefly touched on his aspirations regarding the Olympic Games, which were due to start immediately after the Tour. 'In an Olympic year, it's perhaps normal for your thoughts to turn more often to the Games than to another race, but for me, this year is my very first Tour, and I want to be at the top there as well. We are splitting the month of July into two periods, but both are hyper-important. And I'm hyper-ambitious about both.'

Remco made absolutely no secret of his ambition. Returning to *Het Laatste Nieuws* for a moment: 'I won the Vuelta '22, and was ready to win the Giro '23. If you extend that line... It would be amazing, a huge dream come true. But: it is and will remain my first Tour, one giant voyage of discovery. First, let me learn *how* I should ride the Tour de France and compete for the prizes. My initial goal is a stage win because then I'll have had a stage victory in each of the Grand Tours. And, of course, I'm starting with ambitions for the overall grading. But I don't want to saddle the staff and my teammates with immense pressure. In that sense, I think a top five position in Nice is more realistic. That would already be fantastic. That would give me something on which to build for the future.'

In the weeks leading up to the Tour, while enjoying a fresh espresso in the shade of the Schepdaal church, Patrick had said: 'The Tour? Let's just wait and see how it pans out. I know Remco will do his best, as always. I just hope he doesn't come up against anything in the final stretch of the preparations.' Patrick – and Agna and Oumi – will be stunned by one amazing event after another in July.

On Saturday, 29 June 2024, the day the Tour started in Florence (Italy), the newspapers made a major splash again. In the pull-out supplements – no less than 16 pages to keep! – the reporters on the ground were lyrical in their wording, as if they had a premonition that great things were in the offing: 'Is Remco Evenepoel starting with no ambitions for the overall classification? Don't you believe it. Here are gathered the best riders in the world. Together, Evenepoel, Primož Roglič, Jonas Vingegaard, and Tadej Pogačar form the Big Four of modern cycling. For one, the lead-up was a bit easier than for the others. But there wasn't one who wanted to miss out this time. And so, to the dismay of its critics, the Tour de France remains the biggest cycling race in the world.' And this is how the newspapers concluded: 'Today in Florence, a bona fide Tour de Force begins.'

That was no lie.

21

'REMCO DEMONSTRATED HOW MUCH EFFORT HE IS PUTTING INTO AERODYNAMICS. REMCO, *KING OF THE TIME TRIAL!*'

L'Équipe, the French sports newspaper *par excellence*, pulled all the stops out for the 'Le Grand Départ' of the 111th edition of the Tour. They had created an extra-thick magazine in the editorial office, filled with nostalgic photos and stories, entirely dedicated to the achievements of Eddy Merckx, who in 1974, exactly a half century ago, had claimed his fifth and final Tour victory. And there was another special edition, about the Olympic Games – '*Tout ce qu'il faut savoir pour suivre les Jeux Olympiques d'été!*' (Everything you need to know to follow the Summer Olympics). And then the Tour took place first, in a singular edition, from Florence to Nice. Paris had to prepare for the Games, which after all were due to start on 26 July, a mere five days after the end of the Tour. In short: it was time for a sporting summer to end all sporting summers.

Romain Bardet won the first stage and took the yellow jersey. Immediately a great leaving present for the humble Frenchman who was retiring from racing. The stage winners after that stage were: Kévin Vauquelin, Biniam Girmay, Tadej Pogačar, Marc Cavendish (his 35th stage victory! A record! Just one more than Eddy Merckx!), and Dylan Groenewegen.

And then it was Friday, 5 July. The seventh stage was held between Nuits-Saint-Georges and Gevrey-Chambertin: an individual time trial over 25 kilometres. Remco was fully aware of what lay ahead; he had studied the time trial course inch by inch. Every bend, every straight section, every irregularity, every bump was imprinted in his mind. You know how the race unfolded that day: Remco won, needing exactly 28'52" and 19 hundredths to complete the distance. That was 12 seconds and 36 hundredths less than Pogačar, who finished second. Roglič finished third, 34 seconds behind, Vingegaard came fourth at 37 seconds, and Victor Campenaerts took fifth at 52 seconds. Remco had claimed his first win in the Tour de France – his initial goal was accomplished. Although 12 seconds may not have seemed like a huge gap to his competitors, the cycling world was full of admiration for Remco's achievement. In the international commentary that quickly appeared on the worldwide web, journalists looked beyond the bare numbers. Their main topic of conversation was about the way Remco sat on the bike, how he streamlined his way to victory. *L'Équipe* reported that Remco was the 'roi du chrono', the king of the time trial. The sports newspaper released a podcast and waxed lyrical about Remco's posture on the bike. They said it was poetry in motion: what he demonstrated during those 25 kilometres was proof of how focused he was on aerodynamics. They also noted something remarkable: namely that Remco's understanding of aerodynamics was a result of his background in football. Because of that, he is more flexible, more fluid, and able to adopt postures that others cannot. Cyclingnews, the website that compiles all the news, reports, and coverage on cycling, put it this way: 'Remco Evenepoel announced himself fully at the Tour de France as he seared to a maiden stage win on debut at cycling's biggest race in the stage 7 time trial, outpowering race leader Tadej Pogačar, despite thinking he had suffered a late puncture. The Belgian "aero-bullet" attacked every inch of the 25.3 km route as the Tour headed through the stunning Burgundy vineyards, beating Pogačar in second by only 12 seconds' – From that moment on, Remco was considered a genuine contender for the Tour win, having taken his first stage victory in such a dominant fashion, outperforming Tadej. However, towards the end, he had the fright of his life when it appeared he had a flat tyre (though it turned out to be just an odd noise from the roadside). Every inch of the course was attacked by 'aero-bullet' Remco, as he passed through the beautiful vineyards of Burgundy. The people at Cyclingnews had noticed something else: 'While he wasn't in his ITT World Champion's jersey as the leader of the young rider's classification, the rainbow accents were all over his kit and bike as he ripped through the course, proving he is every bit the best time trialist in the world' – Remco wasn't wearing his world champion's jersey because he was leading the young rider classification, so he had to race in the white jersey. But everything about Remco, both on and around him, bore witness to his status as the world champion, as indicated by the rainbow accents on his bike. In short, the site concluded, Remco was simply the best time trialist in the world.

Tadej Pogačar had a 33-second lead over Remco in the general classification after the time trial. Jonas Vingegaard was in third position at 1'15". The Tour had truly begun now.

22

'REMCO'S QUALITIES ARE ALSO IN HIS DNA. SO: CREDIT MUST GO TO HIS FATHER AND MOTHER.'

Biniam Girmay won the eighth stage, Anthony Turgis the ninth.

After that came the first rest day in the 2024 Tour de France. By now, it was 8 July.

What effect does a rest day have on the riders? Is it really a good thing to have a break? Won't it upset the riders' rhythm? Or are the riders' bodies really desperate for a rest after more than a week. Yannick Balk is a sports and performance psychologist. He completed his PhD at the Eindhoven University of Technology on topics such as mental stress, resilience, and recovery in athletes (and their coaches). Yannick worked for a time at the University of Amsterdam and with Team DSM, the precursor to what became Team dsm-firmenich-PostNL in 2024. He now works for Royal Netherlands Marechaussee – the Dutch military constabulary responsible for border control. Over an early morning coffee, Yannick Balk gave us some insight into what goes on in the head (and the legs) of Remco and the other top riders.

'OK, let's consider a rest day in the Tour,' he says. And Yannick asks himself the question: 'Is it a good thing, that break in a Grand Tour?' He talks about the programmes on TV – in the Netherlands *De Avondetappe*, in Flanders *Vive le Vélo* – and the topic they always cover during the rest day: 'They ask the riders what they get up to on their day off. One rider says he'll still put in three hours on the bike, while another mentions that he'll spend the day reading and relaxing by the pool. You then realise that it very much depends on the rider himself: it's up to him what he does. From the physiological and the body's perspective, the rest day is actually quite beneficial. After three weeks of tough and strenuous effort, that break can really do some good. Mentally, though, it's a different story. When a rider is in the zone, they want to stay there. A rest day can have a detrimental effect on this. Even the mere thought that a rest day could be detrimental leaves the rider 1-0 down in his head.' It's what Yannick Balk designates as the nocebo effect: a negative expectation with no real reason behind it – in contrast to the placebo effect, where simply believing something works is sufficient to make it work. The negative effect doesn't necessarily have to be that big: 'Even a 1 or 2 percent decrease the next day can make a difference in a race like the Tour, where every tiny margin counts.

Be that as it may: top riders – like Remco, Tadej, or Jonas – are usually less negatively affected by a rest day. And there is a reason for that: 'It's probably the case that not only is their experience a factor, but so too, and more especially, are the natural qualities they are blessed with, and they have learned to use these qualities to trim the tension on a rest day just enough. Due to their intense focus on the sport, they also know exactly when to ease up at the right moment. Taking a break from what they do is helpful. Because the next day, when they have to perform again, they do so with more drive, with more motivation. Remco has a strong mindset, as several people mentioned in this book – 'That boy has a head on his shoulders'. What is that though, a strong mindset? Yannick Balk laughs and says: 'That's a good question. I wish I had a clear answer to it. Then of course I'd be able to train and develop the perfect mindset. But anyway, based on what I read about him, I think Remco does indeed have a strong mindset. But Remco possesses a huge amount of intuition, a strong inner motivation. You can see this clearly in time trials: he can push himself to the limit, going beyond the pain barrier, because he *wants* to do it. Remco definitely does that with his mindset, this is what drives him to ride so hard. But another decisive factor is also involved: the qualities he has are in part an inheritance, they're in his very DNA. So: credit must go to his father and mother. In short: Remco is inherently capable of everything he does. He has, however, further developed that over the years. While still a footballer, it was already evident that he had the ability for the kind of achievements he now produces in cycling. As a footballer too, he did very well.'

We should discuss the chicken and egg dilemma here in this context: which comes first? In other words, is Remco so good because he has a strong mindset? Or does he have a strong mindset because he is so good? 'That's an interesting question,' says Balk. Because: 'The jury is still out among the scientists on that one. It's the so-called debate about nature versus nurture: is a person good at something because they have the inherent talent for it (nature), or because it has been shaped by their up-bringing and environment (nurture)? But whether or not you continue to develop that talent always plays a role. And here again, inheritance also plays a part. I think all of this comes together in Remco: he has a strong mindset, the talent for athletic achievements, and he does something with it. See: that's how you become an elite cyclist.'

There's yet another factor that helps explain Remco's development, says the sports and performance psychologist: 'The later someone seriously takes up a sport, the more likely they are to persevere with it. Sometimes the motivation simply disappears, and sometimes athletes get into in a rut. And then they give up, or they no longer have the resilience to continue developing. Remco was into football first and that plays to his advantage. I think he's far from done with racing.' The expert considers further: 'Perhaps Remco just needs to practise a bit of patience for the time being. But it's quite possible that there is still much more to come. It could just be that he wins the Tour de France.'

Later in this book, dear reader, you will learn more about Remco's achievements after the Tour – at the Olympic Games, for example. As you already know, he won two gold medals there. There was no question of Remco suffering from loss of motivation then. He was still able to keep that focus going for a few days. And, Yannick Balk goes on to add: 'I hope that after that, he at least had a chance to celebrate, that he took it easy for a little while. Are you saying he spent a few days away with his wife? Look, those days off, that's great. He put pressure on himself in June, July, and early August to perform. But he also chose to switch off that focus for a while, only to reapply the same intensity later on and then become world time trial champion.'

Father Patrick already mentioned that Remco, Mathieu, Wout, and Tadej are like-minded: top performers in both mind and body. 'That's very true,' says the sports and performance psychologist. 'They understand each other, they're all about the same age, although Mathieu and Wout are a shade older. But still, what stands out to me when I see them race is that they still treat cycling as a kind of game, even though it's also a brutally tough profession for them. Cycling is still their playground, so to speak. That's a healthy mental attitude. They take it absolutely seriously, they're not just messing around. On the contrary, they sacrifice more for it than anyone else. The only difference is that they also do other things that are even more fun. That keeps them fresh. Moreover, these top athletes seem to genuinely wish each other the victories. That's wonderful.' And that's something Patrick Evenepoel had picked up on as well, as you've already read: those guys who work so hard also enjoy themselves – those are the true champions.

Sports psychologist Yannick Balk goes on to add: 'We've talked about Remco the athlete. But it's also important to look at things from a broader perspective, at his parents, his coaches, his team. They provide the space that Remco needs to perform. They don't get in his way. They are not obsessive about it, so they don't deplete his energy. He doesn't have parents that push him. Remco doesn't seem to have an entourage team around him that compels him to deliver results. He's not on duty 24/7.'

After the rest day, the riders had to tackle the mountains again, conserving their energy, pushing themselves to the limit, to the summit of the pass, to the line just beyond the final hairpin bend, and not one metre further. Yannick laughs, he understands what's going on in such nerve-wracking moments: 'The brain constantly uses information to assess how much longer an effort needs to be sustained and how harmful that is. Is the finish line 5 kilometres away, for example? Or 200 metres? The brain processes that information; that's how much further the rider has to maintain maximum effort. After that, it's all over. A familiar wisecrack in that sense is: if you don't drop down dead after the finish line – figuratively speaking – then you could have pushed harder.' And, concludes Yannick Balk: 'Anyone riding for the overall classification, the yellow jersey, or the podium, stays motivated. And lasts longer. Remco is such a person.'

23

'THAT
MOUNTAIN IS
UNFORGIVING.
ALWAYS! THAT
PASS IS A
MONSTER.'

On 13 July 2024, the fourteenth stage of the Tour de France was held in the Pyrenees. The riders had to race from Pau to Pla d'Adetover, a distance of 151.9 kilometres.

Pla d'Adet and Saint-Lary-Soulan, the village at the foot of the pass, are mythical names in the history of the Tour de France. The mountain only made its eleventh appearance in the 2024 Tour, even so there have been heroic scenes to admire on the occasions of the ten previous climbs. Even in the first edition in 1974 – thus a half-century before 2024 – some spectacular action was already presented. Raymond Poulidor – Mathieu van der Poel's grandfather – made a bold move in 1974, attacking Eddy Merckx's dominance. Poupou, as the affable Frenchman was affectionately known, had never managed to wear the yellow jersey in his long career, not even for a single day. By the way, it would never happen for him, he would forever remain the man who never wore the yellow jersey – as time went on, he became the *chouchou*, or darling of the cycling fans, perhaps for the very fact that he never got to wear it. People love an underdog.

In 1974, Poulidor won at Pla d'Adet, with more than a minute's lead over Eddy Merckx. Stunning footage exists of his journey to glory. Those images are somewhat jerky and grainy for they haven't entirely withstood the test of time – even images grow old. The French commentators following in Raymond's wake were enthusiastic, almost lyrical. Daniël Pautrat was the star reporter for TF1, the French television channel; he was *la voix du Tour*, the man who first followed the riders in the car when things were still calm during a stage. Legend has it that the car was a Matra Simca Bagheera, named after the panther from *The Jungle Book*. But as soon as things heated up in the race and people wanted to know more precisely what was happening, Pautrat would step out of his Matra and take up pillion position on the motorcycle. From that moment on, he was right there in the race. He manoeuvred himself beside, behind, and in front of the riders. Pautrat was part of the Tour, a star amidst the stars. '*Cette folle ambiance*,' said Pautrat, the atmosphere was electrifying. Raymond Poulidor had just a few hundred more metres to climb, the road surface was poor, the bend to the right, past the sign for the last 150 metres, extremely steep uphill, and then the final straight – Pla d'Adet was a monstrous climb – 'Raymond Poulidor wins a magnificent victory, he's 38 years old!' echoed the unalloyed admiration for Raymond's triumph. In the twilight of his cycling years, Poulidor was the strongest man in the race. Merckx finished fifth, 1'48" behind, but in the end he went on to win his fifth Tour de France that year. That turned out to be his last one. Was the beating Eddy took from Poulidor in 1974 a foretaste of what a year later would truly mark the start of when his empire began to crumble?

In any case: in 1974, Pla d'Adet had already earned its place in the annals of the Tour de France. What did people think about that mountain? It was extremely tough and quintessentially Pyrenean. Because – and it's a fact – the Pyrenees are different from the Alps. Experienced riders point out that the passes in the Pyrenees may be shorter than those in the Alps, but at the same time, they are steeper. You have to climb steeply in the hairpin bends, which, to make matters worse, are often in poor condition, the paths are narrower, and the heat is more scorching, more oppressive – even discounting the possibility of a thunderstorm.

In short: the Pyrenees are a nightmare, and Pla d'Adet even more so.

Two years after Raymond Poulidor, Lucien Van Impe unleashed his demons on the way to the mountain village of Saint-Lary-Soulan. It was on 10 July 1976 that Lucien made his move, and as of 2024, he is still the last Belgian to have won the Tour de France. That Saturday was yet another hot, sunny day. In the hit parade for that day, in Belgium, Lucien's homeland, 'Rocky' by Don Mercedes was number 1, a sentimental song from the Netherlands. (The best songs of that summer were at number 4 – 'Arms of Mary' by Sutherland Brothers & Quiver – and number 6 – 'Show Me the Way' by Peter Frampton. Or rather, that's not actually true: the best number was at number 7: 'This Melody' by Julien Clerc – *'Cette*

*mélodie, d'eau salée en de mélancolie – dans ton pays – elle te revient par-
fois – comme ça, voilà, comme ça'.* It was the embodiment of France, in
musical form.)

Lucien Van Impe had a plan for that Saturday, 10 July. He was going to
reclaim the yellow jersey he'd lost two days earlier – or rather, had given
up, as strategically that had seemed a better idea at the time. He decided to take the jersey once and for all that day. And he succeeded, in spectacular fashion. His biggest rival, Joop Zoetemelk, trailed by minutes,
as Lucien tore the peloton apart. That evening in his hotel room, when
Lucien received the package containing his fresh new yellow jersey –
made of wool – he was taken aback: the package also included the day's
communiqué, a summary of fines, withdrawals, and the stage results.
Lucien read that the Italian Alessio Antonini had crossed the finish line
in 52nd place, 28 minutes and 30 seconds behind. Following behind
Alessio, there were another 43 riders. And all of them were outside the
time limit, more than 40 minutes behind. According to the rules, they
all had to go home. But discussions continued way into the night about
the issue: surely you couldn't have the Tour entering Paris with such a
small peloton in just over a week? No, that simply couldn't be allowed
to happen. After much discussion, Jacques Goddet and Félix Lévitan,
the directors of the Tour de France, decided that the entire peloton
would be allowed to continue in the race.

Pla d'Adet had lived up to its reputation of being a monster.
That mountain is eternally unforgiving.
As indeed it was on Saturday, 13 July 2024.

24

IN *L'ÉQUIPE* IT
SAID THAT JONAS
VINGEGAARD
THANKED REMCO
FOR TAKING HIM TO
THE FINISH LINE

On Saturday, 13 July 2024, Don Mercedes was long forgotten, although sometimes you could still hear him singing about Rocky and the tragic life of his girlfriend, their child, and the premature departure from life on a radio station full of *oldies*, but *goldies*. Now, in 2024, it was other songs that graced the charts: *'Espresso'* by Sabrina Carpenter, for example – *'Now he's thinkin' bout me every night, oh!'*

The first Pyrenean stage in the Tour brought the riders from Pau to Pla d'Adet. The first peak to be climbed was that other legendary mountain: the Tourmalet, an hors catégorie climb. The riders had to ascend it from the most difficult side – a 19-kilometre climb with an average gradient of 7.4%. After that came the Hourquette d'Ancizan (8.2 kilometres, average 5.1%). Then the riders were less than 30 kilometres from the finish, heading towards Saint-Lary-Soulan and Pla d'Adet. Remco showed his maturity there. It became increasingly clear – especially in the comments on radio and television, in the papers and on various digital channels. Well, Tadej Pogačar had been phenomenally strong, he had conquered with ease, and Jonas Vingegaard had responded to those devastating attacks, causing Remco to lose his second place in the provisional overall standings. But Remco had set something in motion. Somehow or other, the journalists covering the race sensed a kind of turning point. Marc Ghyselinck, the senior cycling reporter of *Het Laatste Nieuws*, published a clear analysis that evening of Saturday, 13 July, on his newspaper's website. Amongst what was a long article, this was written: 'Follow, follow, follow. Evenepoel had summarised this plan of his for the first Pyrenees stage to Pla d'Adet in three words on Friday in Pau. In week one, on the Col du Galibier, Evenepoel decided that Tadej Pogačar and Jonas Vingegaard were in a different league. More experience in the high mountains, more power as well. Evenepoel may have won the Vuelta a España, but the fact that Pogačar and Vingegaard had each won the Tour twice is on a different level, he understood.' After this introduction, the journalist went on, writing: 'Evenepoel is not the type of rider who often lets others take the initiative. He prefers to attack himself. In this Tour de France, he's in the process of reinventing himself. This is how it goes:

Pogačar attacks, Vingegaard reacts immediately, and Evenepoel then finds his own pace. It's a matter of self-awareness and respect for his opponents. As (team leader) Tom Steels says: "He finds his own limits and then decides not to exceed them." After two weeks of the Tour de France, this strategy brought him to second place in the general classification. That was on Saturday morning at the start in Pau, where the Tour was only now about to truly begin, with two stages in the Pyrenees on Saturday and Sunday. And the week after, two major Alpine stages and a grand finale with a final time trial in Nice. Evenepoel has already passed the first Pyrenean test with flying colours. Once again, Pogačar attacked while Vingegaard immediately responded, and once again, Evenepoel tried, in his own way, to stay as close as possible to the big two.' And then the man from the newspaper brought up a factor that has already been discussed throughout this book: Remco's mindset – or, in other words: 'There was a touch of bravado when Evenepoel recounted the story of the stage. "When Pogačar attacked, I was more or less boxed in between Matteo Jorgenson and Mikel Landa. I wasn't able to respond immediately. Had I been so then I would have got right on Vingegaard's wheel and might have been able to follow him to the top." Evenepoel closed the gap on Vingegaard, but paid for the effort when he had to let the Dane go 3 kilometres from the top. The difference between him and Pogačar at the top was 1'10", and he lost 31 seconds to Vingegaard. Evenepoel continued his story: "Three kilometres from the top, there was a slight downhill section, and after that, I struggled to maintain the rhythm. But I don't think Jonas gained much on me during that section. Today I showed that I'm not that far off Vingegaard's level," he said. "Despite the fact he dropped me. On Sunday, I may be the one to drop him." So, that was clear, and with it an end to the unquestioning respect for the two-time Danish Tour winner.

Remco had – all of a sudden, it seemed – taken up a more prominent position in the ranks of the elite riders' peloton. This became crystal clear at the end of the nineteenth stage. On 19 July, the riders rode up to the top of Isola 2000 – that's right: Remco's training area.

It makes for fascinating reading to include *L'Équipe* here and see what the newspaper wrote in its Saturday edition of 20 July, after – once again – a remarkable performance by Pogačar. There was a large, full-page photo of the Slovenian on the cover, wearing his yellow jersey and bowing in a kind of self-reverential pose: 'Look at me, people. This is what I've accomplished.' The large-lettered caption over the photo read: '*Le coup de grâce* – Tadej had delivered the fatal blow; it sounded softer in French than in other languages.

On page three was the official result: the stage from Embrun to Isola 2000, over 144.6 kilometres. The average speed of winner Pogačar was 35.55 kilometres per hour. In completing the route, he'd ridden for 4 hours, 4 minutes, and 3 seconds. What was striking were places five and six: Remco and Jonas Vingegaard rolled over the line together at 1'42". A bit further inside the newspaper, Remco warranted half a page plus a photo. The headline of the piece: '*Jonas m'a remercié de l'avoir emmené*' – Jonas thanked Remco for taking him along in his slipstream to the finish line. In the photo, Remco was riding on the right, his white jersey of the leader in the young rider classification slightly open. His face looked quite fresh, somewhat mischievous. Remco extended his hand to Jonas, who was deeply hunched over in his polka-dot jersey. The newspaper detailed what had occurred in the stage: 'Evenepoel accelerated, climbing at his own pace. Vingegaard chose not to follow Pogačar, then resisted until the end to the rhythm of the Brabançonne. The pat on the back followed by the handshake exchanged between the two at the finish line signalled an armistice. Remco added to that: 'He thanked me for taking him with me, and there's no shame in crossing the line with a double Tour winner.' According to *L'Équipe*, it was the image of a ceasefire between two great riders – Jonas and Remco. And, as duly noted in the same columns, it was also the story of two men who had travelled a shared journey, after their severe crash in the Basque Country, just a few months previously. For them, the 2024 Tour de France began on 4 April, during the descent of the Col d'Olaeta, during the Tour of the Basque Country, where a treacherous turn sent them crashing to the ground. Pneumothorax, pulmonary contusion, cracked sternum, and fractures of the left collarbone and several ribs for Vingegaard. Twelve days in hospital, ten weeks of rehabilitation, and an invisible task to accomplish: digesting the idea that you'd thought you were going to die. For Evenepoel, a fractured shoulder blade and collarbone. While the former burst into tears yesterday, perhaps in an entangled mixture of frustration and accomplishment, the Belgian expressed a controlled satisfaction: "I felt good, everything went according to plan." *L'Équipe* returned to that unfortunate 4th of April, and the crash on that bend. For Remco and Jonas, the Tour had started that day, said the newspaper. For that was when their recovery began after fractures and much hardship – and ended in tears of joy. Cycling is a tough sport. And now, on 19 July, Remco and Jonas had crossed the finish line hand-in-hand; they were riders once again, after all the hardship.

The final podium for the 2024 Tour de France took place in Nice. Tadej Pogačar won the yellow jersey, 6 minutes and 17 seconds ahead of Jonas Vingegaard. Remco finished third – and as best young rider – at 9 minutes and 18 seconds. Having taken part for the first time in the greatest race of all, there he was, standing on the podium.
With one week to go to the Olympic Games.

25

'WE WERE JUST STANDING ALONG THE COURSE. WHEN HE PASSED US, WE KNEW EVERYTHING WAS ALRIGHT. ON THE WAY HOME, ON THE TRAIN, THAT'S WHEN IT REALLY SANK IN.'

The Olympic Games are the pinnacle of sporting experience. Every four years, the best athletes from all around the world enter the arena to compete for gold, silver, and bronze. The names of those who have stood there on the podium are etched in history. Abebe Bikila, the Ethiopian who won the marathon barefoot in 1960, and Dick Fosbury, the American who jumped 2.24 metres in the high jump at the 1968 Olympics in Mexico City. Nothing special per se, not a world record by any means, but Dick's technique was something else. He jumped backwards, a new method which no one had used before – the birth of the Fosbury Flop. Names to conjure with, such as Bob Beamon, who in 1968, also in Mexico City, long-jumped 8.90 metres just before a thunderstorm broke out, no one had ever reached that far before. And Mark Spitz, in 1972 in Munich, seven-time gold medallist in swimming, a record for the American with the moustache, and Michael Phelps, Spitz's fellow countryman, who won 23 (!) golds in swimming, making him the most successful Olympian ever in the Summer Games – how can someone be so good at what he does? Standout names like Nadia Comaneci, Olga Korbut, Simone Biles, and Nina Derwael, on a variety of gymnastic apparatus in a blend of grace, beauty, and style. And Dave Wottle, the rather slow runner in the 800 metres in Munich – or so it seemed anyway – the man with the white cap on his head, ran in the final – quite literally – behind the other athletes, trailing behind them, until he moved forward and won. And Ivo Van Damme, another track athlete, who won two silvers in Montreal in 1976. A great future awaited Ivo, he could have become Olympic champion in the 800 and 1500 metres, he was that good – until an accident on the motorway in the south of France robbed him of his life, a sad event that led to the Ivo Van Damme Memorial being created in honour of him. And athletes like Carl Lewis, Usain Bolt, swimmer Fredje Deburghgraeve, and Nafi Thiam, as agile as a gazelle, so fantastic in the heptathlon, three-time gold medallist in Rio (2016), Tokyo (2021), and Paris (2024).

Famous names indeed. Men and women to whom people look up. Men and women who have entered the Pantheon of Sport. They are the greatest, the gods of sport – and that's no exaggeration. Remco has belonged there since the summer of 2024 as well. In Paris, he became an Olympic champion twice – in the individual time trial and in the road race. Here, dear reader, you will find the account of two days at the cutting edge, related by those most closely involved.

'We were in Paris, during the time trial,' recount Patrick and Agna. 'We were there with our close friends.' Patrick and Agna were standing exactly 1.8 kilometres from the finish, simply next to the course. 'On the street, at a spot where we saw Remco pass by twice, the riders reached that spot and then rode back from there. A great spot to stand, for sure.'

'We followed the race on our phones,' they say.
'And immediately, we could see that everything was going well.'
'At just under two kilometres in, Remco came through with a three-second lead over Ganna.'
'That pedal cadence, it was spot on. If it continued like this, then it would work out fine. We could tell that everyone was nervous. It was raining; it was a matter of staying upright. Remco simply couldn't afford to fall now.'

During the Tour de France a few weeks earlier, Remco received a lot of praise for his posture on the bike – '*roi du chrono*', is how *L'Équipe* described it, as we mentioned before. That Remco would, before long, be called 'aerobullet' came as no surprise. Let's refer back for a moment to Kevin De Weert, the coach who brought Remco into the climb project of Belgian Cycling in 2017. 'That Remco adopts such a perfectly aerody namic position on the bike is actually quite logical,' he says. 'Remco wanted exactly that, such a streamlined position. It was natural for him to concentrate his attention on that. He constantly searched for videos of riders doing time trials and watched them over and over again. He picked up the right things from them and put them into practice himself.' Patrick Verschueren remembers that too: 'Yeah,' he says. 'And then, of course, you become an aerobullet.' Kevin De Weert laughs and adds:

'Remco's posture, that's something to behold, even when he's just riding in the peloton or in a leading group. When he's riding up front and you're on his wheel, you're definitely not out of the wind. On his wheel, you're exposed to all the wind. It's no joke, you know.' And that term, or nickname – or what do you call something like that, the aerobullet? It was Yves Lampaert, Remco's cheerful team mate – 'I'm just a farmer's son from Belgium...' – who first used the word, and that happened on 10 June 2021. On that day, Yves was in the hot seat after the time trial from Knokke to Knokke in the Tour of Belgium. He was on track to win that 11.2-kilometre time trial. However, then Remco turned up. No, Yves had said, I'm not going to make it. And: 'Remco, that's an aerobullet.' Remco did indeed win, with a two-second lead over Lampaert – it was his first victory after his serious fall in Lombardy. Exactly 300 days had passed since his last victory. Three days later, Remco also became the overall winner of the Tour of Belgium. And he had earned himself a nickname: he was no longer just the kid from Schepdaal, the youngster from Schepdaal. He was now also the aerobullet, the man who rode his bike in one smooth motion. Remarkable, isn't it? For wasn't Remco the rider who – especially in the early days of his cycling career – fell off so often and couldn't steer?

'Well,' says his father Patrick, 'that's an image people have of Remco that I want to correct. It is indeed true that he had that serious crash in Limburg, right at the start of his career. And he fell in Bergen, Norway, as well. But the entire Belgian team was floored there.' But, says Patrick: 'Remco ended up with that label. Strange, really. People said he originated from football and therefore couldn't ride a bike. I'm still surprised to find that it's a label that Remco may never shake off. Yes, it's true that as a junior, Remco almost never rode in the peloton. But no, it's not true that he avoided it because he was too scared to ride in a group. He did that because he was so strong. He wanted to race, he wanted to attack. If he'd been afraid, he would have been dropped. If he'd been afraid, he would have braked. And that didn't happen.' There was another thing too: Remco couldn't descend. But, says Patrick: 'Did you watch him in action at the world championship time trials in Zurich? National coach Sven Vanthourenhout said afterwards that, while following in the car, he had shut his eyes during that incredibly difficult and dangerous descent. He didn't dare watch how Remco was handling it there. No, 'says Patrick once again: 'In the end, once you get a label like that, it's impossible to dislodge it.'

Back to the Olympic time trial and father Evenepoel's account...
'We first saw Remco when he stepped out of the van at the Belgian Olympic House, holding his gold medal. We hadn't heard anything about him all the time prior to that. We hadn't even received a message from Remco. Remco, and Wout who had won bronze, were being pulled from pillar to post, with no control over what was happening to them, such was the scale of the Olympic Games. Remco and Wout still hadn't eaten after the ceremonial protocol. What's more they hadn't even been able to shower yet. But still, the Games were only on their first day, and Belgium had already won two medals. That was bound to give a boost to the entire delegation from Remco's home country.'

And there was no winding down for Remco. He didn't ease up at all. Remco was intent on performing in the road race a week later as well. The absence of any hint of losing focus, according to Remco's father, was due to what he had mentioned earlier in this book: it all took place in Remco's mind. 'Once Remco makes a decision, he goes for it. And Remco had definitely decided that he would stay focused for another week after the time trial. He wanted to become Olympic champion in the road race as well. His *mind* simply tells him to do it, and then his legs do what they are instructed to do: to win, or at least attempt to.'

The road race at the Olympics went perfectly for the Belgian team on Saturday, 3 August. A strong leading group had formed, the crowd was ecstatic, and the atmosphere in the streets of Paris was tingling with tension. 'The race would have been completely different if Wout van Aert, Mathieu van der Poel, Matteo Jorgenson, and Julian Alaphilippe, who had gone in pursuit, had actually got in touch with that leading group,' says Patrick. 'It would have been interesting to see what would have happened if those top riders had been able to join the first group.' But Wout, Matteo, Mathieu, and Julian failed in their attempt. Actually, there was nothing surprising about that, recounts Patrick. 'I think Wout and Mathieu weren't having their best of days,' he says. 'Otherwise, they would have caught up with the leading group. And then the race would have been decided.' Due to the way the race unfolded, Remco was in a comfortable position: he didn't have to do anything himself, as his fellow countryman Wout van Aert was trying catch the leading group. And if that failed to happen, Remco had complete freedom (and up to then, he hadn't wasted a single unnecessary pedal stroke).

Remco had a specific point in mind where he would try for the first time, where he would put the proverbial cat among the pigeons. That point? The climb after Montmartre, right in the centre of Paris, 78 kilometres from the finish. That's where Remco wanted – if possible – to break open the race. Patrick, grinning all over: 'And that's what happened too.' He takes a sip of his coffee and says: 'Did I know about that plan in advance? Nope. But if you know how the team around Remco has been riding for the past two or three years, then you knew it would likely unfold in this way.' Anyway, Remco's plan worked perfectly. He opened up a gap and was on his way to his second Olympic gold medal in a week.

'We were standing in the Belgian café on the course,' says Patrick.
'It had a giant screen. People could following everything on it.'
But, says Patrick: 'I was following it on my mobile.'
'And I noticed that the images on the phone and on the giant screen were out of synch.'
'On my phone, Remco was already a kilometre further along the course.'
'I saw that he had a flat tyre.'
'By the time I realised that, people suddenly saw it on the giant screen also.'

That was a stand-out moment, says Patrick: 'People from the press had already been following Agna and me for quite some time, and now we were surrounded by them. We just wanted to watch the race quietly, but all that crowd, all those journalists, the cameras, and then the flat tyre.' Was there panic? Oh, panic? What is panic? 'You can't change the situation,' Patrick says. 'Things are what they are.' And – besides – Remco had a very good lead. And yet: 'We were quite happy that the support vehicle was there quickly, with national coach Sven Vanthourenhout and mechanic Kurt Roose.'

Remco stopped on the left-hand side of the road.
He got off his bike.
Clapped his hands – quick, quick, quick.
'Then Remco uttered the famous words,' says Patrick.
'Bike!'
'Bike!!'
Remco got his bike, and the lead was large enough.

At the finish line, Remco stopped, dismounted from his bike, stretched his arms wide into the air, his head tilted towards the heavens – for a moment of heavenly joy, indeed. The image of that moment instantaneously became iconic and worthy of being featured on the cover of this book. 'S-Works' was prominently displayed on Remco's bike. It was the name of the top brand of Specialized, Remco's bike sponsor.

'We've been with Remco since he was a boy. Every major race he's won, from his first World Championship as a junior to his incredible Olympic double in Paris, has been with Specialized. Remco's so much more than an athlete we sponsor, he's family,' says Mike Sinyard from California in the USA. Mike Sinyard, CEO of Specialized until 2022, is a man in his seventies, who founded his company in 1974. When he started up his business, the idea was about 'specialized bicycle components, to do exactly what the name suggests: sell high-quality bike parts'. His company's name made it clear what it did: it sold bike parts – parts that he also imported from Europe. But parts on their own? No, Mike didn't settle for that, his sights were on bigger things. By the late 1970s, complete bicycles were being produced, and in the following decade, mountain bikes were introduced with great success. Mike grew up in San Diego in the fifties and sixties. The Sinyard family was not well off. 'We didn't have a lot', as he puts it. 'My sister and I were a little bit like outcasts.' He calls himself and his sister 'the hillbillies in the city', children of a more modest background. Mother worked as a cleaner in houses, father – a machinist in the US Navy – and Mike fixed whatever needed repairing in homes, they did whatever jobs needed doing anywhere – 'We fixed things'. It was a simple life, they never went to restaurants – 'Do you know what the best restaurant is?' father would ask his children. 'Do you know where the best restaurant is? 'It's called "Home".' But now, looking back, Mike is able to appreciate that ordinary, simple life, he knows where he comes from. He left school when he was 16 – it wasn't going too well there – and he left home as well, 'to sell things at the flea-market'. But a year later, he decided to go back to school and did jobs at the airport. He even earned a pilot's licence there – 'Hey, I did something!' In the meantime, Mike had already started cycling, and his father kept busy repairing and doing up things. Even when Mike was just eight years old, they would assemble things together. And that led Mike to start buying bikes and bike parts at the flea markets he was so familiar with and then, 'putting them together'. Mike repainted the bikes so that they looked great, and it was the beginning of it all: 'That was the spark of the interest in bicycles.' He travelled to Europe where the parts were of better quality, where cycling culture was more deeply embedded in people's hearts and souls, and saw that he could fill a gap in the market in America with European parts: 'What a gap! It would be really big.' In 1972, Mike graduated, and spent his first year doing odd jobs, he'd never made so much money before. Until the school where he worked let him go. It was time to take the leap, it was now 1974. He started importing from Europe, going from one shop to another and selling what he had to offer. Specialized was in business. The rest is history.

Mike Sinyard offers more insight into the connection between himself, Specialized, and Remco: 'We share a passion and commitment to improve, to win, to innovate. Together we make each other better and reach higher levels of performance than we could ever do alone. Remco's already made history, and we know he's just getting better. Specialized and Remco will be partners for life. Remco, his wife Oumi, his mom and dad, the support team around him, they are all part of the Specialized family. We couldn't be prouder that Remco chooses to ride with us and our future together couldn't be brighter.' These are loving words. And they are well-deserved, expressing not only admiration but also gratitude for the journey they have travelled together: they connected through their passion for innovation, their determination to win, and their commitment to always strive to be better. Together, they achieve more than they could on their own, with Remco being the inspiration behind it all – this is a partnership for life. Mike Sinyard rounds it off like this: 'The future can only look brighter, and Remco has already made history.'

Remco was now Olympic champion on the road. Oumi was waiting for him at the finish.
Patrick and Agna downed a celebratory glass in the Belgian Café, where they were showered with congratulations.
The next day, on the train on the way home, that's when it sank in: 'We're parents to an Olympic champion. And now people also want selfies with us, with the parents of the winner. All of a sudden, there were again many changes looming in our lives.'

26

'WE'RE STILL
THE SAME
PEOPLE THOUGH.
WE'RE STILL THE
SAME PEOPLE
WHO LIVE OUR
LIVES FULL GAS
AND WORK HARD,
EACH DAY ANEW.'

Had Agna and Patrick's life indeed changed?

Yes: not many people have a son who stood on the podium at the Tour and won gold medals at the Games. But Agna and Patrick do have such a son.

But no, their life had not changed. Because, as they say: 'We ourselves, we remain the same people, we're still those two self-employed individuals who work hard every day, morning, noon, and night. We're people who live our lives *full gas*. That's still our motto.' But it is the things surrounding them, around Remco and Oumi, that have changed – it's the outside world that has changed over the past weeks, months, and years. 'Suddenly, everyone knows who Remco is, people know who Oumi is, who we are, Patrick and Agna, Remco's parents.' They were people outside of cycling, not part of the cycling community, and this was the case worldwide, people had discovered the Evenepoel family. Messages arrived from China, Japan, Canada, via Instagram and Facebook. Requests for photos arrived from people who had only just started to learn about Remco's story: the story of the footballer who became a cyclist. It was an instantaneous explosion of interest. And then, suddenly, there was also interest from news channel CNN and the *New York Times*, all the way from the United States, and inquiries from Australia. 'There are companies that want Remco to give a speech, or to come and open a new branch. They want him – a young man, still only 24 years old in 2024 – as a motivational speaker to tell CEOs and other managers how they can attain their goals through hard work and focus. For them, Remco is someone with the potential to transcend the sport,' says Patrick. And he goes on to state this: 'Remco's mix of charisma, being both playful and professional in his actions, resonates with people. Someone who also has that, and probably to an even greater extent, is Tadej. He is still more exceptional.' In any case: the two gold medals have had a greater impact – even more than the podium in the Tour. The parents repeats once again: 'Everybody knows Remco now.'

Patrick and Agna fall silent for a moment.

'What that means for us,' they then say.

'Yeah.'

'Yes, for us?'

'There is so much that has been added.'

'We now have to try to think about ourselves again.'

'Ourselves as a family.'

'Take a much-needed rest.'

'And do the things we still need to do.'

'Something quite banal perhaps, like mowing the lawn.'

'Or painting the front of the house.'

'We need to gradually start doing that again.'

'Refurbish the garage, that's another one.'

'Small things.'

'But they accumulate.'

'Yes, a lot is expected of us.'

'And of Remco?'

'And Oumi.'

'Now we have to dare to say: this is just for us.'

'That's something just for us.'

There was still another factor at play. Certainly after the Tour de France, that was the case: after his performances in France, Remco had grown up. Was more mature. At least, that's how others saw it. Somehow or other, a different perception of Remco had begun to take shape in the public's mind. In itself, that was quite remarkable, thinks Patrick Evenepoel. 'Apparently, many people now realise that Remco is different from what they thought. What did they think before? That Remco could be arrogant, for example. Or that he would only think about himself, that it's always a case of me, me, me. It was a label he'd been given from right from the start and just couldn't shake off, for some reason. But Remco is not like that. The image that was presented of him, I always thought it was such a shame.' Patrick and Agna have thought about that a lot. They recognise the situation from Remco's early years as a young footballer at Anderlecht. 'Then those players from the U9 team would arrive at an away game against the weekend's opponent, and the boys were called bigheads. Simply because they played for Anderlecht. But those people didn't know the children. These people knew nothing about their background.

People can react strangely, is what it comes down to.
But now, after three weeks of the Tour, the tide had turned for Remco. After two gold medals in Paris, Remco had become fully embraced in the hearts of the men and women who were thrilled by his success. Suddenly, they had grasped that Remco was a great cyclist with a great character. And what Fred Vandervennet had hoped for earlier had happened in the summer of 2024: Remco had made people dream, he had brought them along on the journey of his incredible accomplishments, and it was a spark of joy that radiated to everyone in Remco's home country.

The image had shifted.
It was time for a new feat.
Because that was what people were now eagerly anticipating.
A feat at the world championship, for example.

27

IT WAS 16:34,
SUNDAY AFTERNOON,
22 SEPTEMBER 2024,
WHEN SOMETHING
STRANGE HAPPENED.

In Zurich, it had been a lovely, sunny day all day. Ideal weather for racing, in short: not too hot, hovering around twenty degrees, with little wind. The conditions were, in other words, nearly perfect. In the early afternoon, just a few hours before Remco was set to mount the starting podium, the women had already completed their World Championship time trial. The Australian Grace Brown – who'd also won a gold medal at the Paris Olympics just a few weeks earlier – had won. The elite mens riders could now prepare for their competition. And Remco was one of the favourites (not to mention that he was also the defending champion). It was a classic textbook course, a route along idyllic roads, with the Lake of Zurich, the Zürichsee, in the background, over a distance of 46.1 kilometres, with 413 metres of elevation gain and a tough climb with a gradient of just over 6%, followed by a steep descent, as if the riders were riding into a black hole. They started at the Oerlikon velodrome, an outdoor track that was built in 1912.

Remco was ready for the battle at 16:34.

His bike was decorated in the gold colours of his Olympic title and looked splendid.

Anyone watching TV saw it all: Remco's chain came off before he had even ridden a metre, before even leaving the starting podium. The viewers – especially Remco's (many) supporters – felt a cold sweat break out: 'No! Remco! What are you doing? 'What's happening?' Barely a minute was left before Remco would start. In the footage, you saw how two mechanics arrived in a hurry and fixed the issue. Momentarily, a cameraman appeared (for a very short while) on the podium, just behind the bike. Remco wasn't too pleased about this, or so it seemed at least – Remco appeared to stretch out an arm towards the man (or woman?) who was filming him far too closely. Whether that's true, dear reader, you'll find out on the last pages of this book. A third mechanic turned up, a second bike was provided. Just 27 seconds were left to go before the start. Then off he went, propelled by adrenaline and ambition.

After 12.5 kilometres – in Maur – Remco had a 6 second and 70 hundredths lead over Ganna.

After 26.6 kilometres – in Uetikon am See – Remco had a 9 second and 20 hundredths lead over Ganna.

After 36.7 kilometres – in Herrliberg – Remco had a 19 seconds lead over Ganna.

After 46.1 kilometres – in Zurich – Remco had a 6 seconds and 43 hundredths lead over Ganna.

Everything had been fixed, and Remco had surged ahead to claim the world title, his second consecutive one. After the race, he had this to say about it: 'Yes, my heart also stood still there at the start. I just briefly pedalled backwards to find my power meter again. Consequently, the chain came off, probably my own fault. That happened to me once before in the Basque Country this year. It's something I should actually stop doing. But, yeah, it happens. These days, we ride with those big chainrings, front chainrings. Everything is so finely adjusted that you can't make mistakes any more. Purely and simply my own fault. Then I take up my starting position, and there's no power meter. So, during that first kilometre, I had to try to find my power meter. I was fiddling with my screen, but I couldn't find it any more. So yes, it was a very frustrating time trial from start to finish. Also, it was very difficult to *pace* myself that way. I think everyone knows that I'm someone who likes to follow my numbers very strictly, and particularly in a time trial like this, that's essential. I heard that I had a six-second lead at the first checkpoint, about nine seconds at the second, and a bit more after the descent, I think. But then, yes, I started to feel it was getting extremely difficult. Those were all the numbers I had the entire time. I wasn't quite sure what I was doing in the final straight. I wanted to make my move there, after the hilly section.'

Remco concluded: 'In view of all the circumstances, probably the most difficult time trial of my life.'

And then, rather matter-of-factly, with a slight smile on his face: 'But in the end, I won, that's the most important thing. And I'm still making a bit of history. Good, right?'

28

BY THE END
OF SEPTEMBER,
THE SUMMER OF
2024 WAS OVER.

In the meantime, the weather had turned, especially in the countries in northern and western Europe. In the preceding week and a half, the Indian summer had lasted just long enough for many to take a final trip to the sea, time for a final glass of rosé in the setting sun. Ordinary people, like you and me, could still enjoy the soothing rays of the sun for a little longer. But now autumn had begun. And the weather wasn't the only thing going in that direction. It had suddenly become grey and dreary in the minds of those involved in the world of cycling too, for on Friday, 27 September, during the live broadcast of the U23 road race at the World Championships, the sad news came through that Muriel Furrer had passed away. The cheerful Swiss girl had started the World Championship in the junior women's race on Thursday, the day before, full of hope and expectations, in her own country, in the vicinity of her own home no less, close to her family and loved ones. That Thursday morning, she crashed heavily, and the brain injury she sustained was severe – too severe. The World Championship was in mourning. Muriel was barely 18 years old.

But in the days that followed, it was race time again in Zurich – life has to go on. Lotte Kopecky was strong and clever again on the first day of the weekend. She became world champion again, for the second year in a row. The Belgian athlete sprinted in the rain, shivering from the cold, to claim the title in the elite women riders' race. A minute later, her compatriot Justine Ghekiere – who in daily life races for Remco's sister team, AG Insurance-Soudal – finished seventh, after a day's hard work in support of her leader Lotte. Justine chirped and laughed and waved and giggled and shivered, so happy for Kopecky, so proud of her own phenomenal race – no one could sweat it out as gracefully as Ghekiere that day.

On Sunday, 29 September, it was time for the climax: that's when the road race title battle for elite men was due to be ridden. Remco was able there to add a crowning achievement to a miraculous summer. After his impressive victory in the time trial a week earlier, he was also one of the top favourites for the road race. In the days leading up to the race, the papers devoted many column inches to their pre-race analysis – they discussed the chances of Mathieu van der Poel, the defending world champion, Primož Roglič, and Tadej Pogačar, 26 years old and – somewhat surprisingly – still never having worn the rainbow jersey. Pogačar could become the third rider in cycling history to win both the Giro, the Tour, and the World Championship in a single year, following in the footsteps of Eddy Merckx in 1974 and the Irishman Stephen Roche in 1987. The Slovenian did indeed achieve that; you may recall how he attacked 100 kilometres from the finish, rode up to the leading group, taking only the Frenchman Pavel Sivakov – Pogačar's teammate at UAE in the regular peloton! – along with him for a few dozen kilometres, and ultimately bowled across the line alone – to take the world championship title. That he initiated a breakaway – the right breakaway – so far from the finish was surprising. But anyway: it happened, and Tadej was simply very strong. He deserved to become world champion at the end of September.

Remco finished fifth, maintaining focus throughout the chase in the group pursuing Pogačar. He still joined the sprint for the medals, but Ben O'Connor (who broke away from that compact group at the end), Mathieu van der Poel, and Toms Skujinš stayed in front of him. Remco rode a fine race. Later on, he had this to say about it: 'It was a crazy move by Tadej, we thought it was suicidal, I was convinced of it. This won't lead anywhere, we thought. I saw him go and was quite optimistic, this wasn't it. But it turned out not to be a crazy move after all. Not normal, but typical Tadej. That's him for you. Based on his fantastic riding this season, he deserves to be world champion.' Remco added with a wink: 'Next year, we'll start racing 200 kilometres from the finish.'

But let's hark back to the days before the 2024 title race: among all the discussions with the favourites about who would win (or not) and the pre-race analyses, there was another contribution that received a lot of attention on Friday, 27 September. On the front page of the sports section of *Het Laatste Nieuws*, the largest Flemish newspaper, there was a big headline: 'Evenepoel to stay at Soudal-Quick-Step.' The sub-headline of the article: 'No transfer despite talks with Red Bull-Bora-Hansgrohe and another team.' That was a somewhat surprising report, as in the past weeks and months, the rumour mill about Remco's move to another team had been in full swing. At various points during the writing of this book, the story of a new team did the rounds, it was discussed over more than one cup of coffee, a few feelers were put out more than once. It seemed plausible that Remco's contract with Patrick Lefevere's team would remain intact, but at the same time, it also seemed just as plausible that Remco would leave, because in many ways, both in press articles and in the corridors of the race, it was whispered (aloud) that the Soudal-Quick Step team was not strong enough to allow Remco to fulfil his ultimate goal – winning the Tour de France. The general feeling was that a strong injection of quality was needed, particularly with the addition of good climbers. The affable Spaniard Mikel Landa had already been welcomed as a newcomer – Landa performed well right from the start in the 2024 Tour de France, working for Remco, not collapsing under pressure, and finishing fifth in the general classification himself. In August 2024, the Frenchman Valentin Paret-Peintre and the German Maximilian Schachmann were recruited – two climbers. In short: Remco's team really seemed to be making an effort to bring in the necessary reinforcements. But there were lingering doubts: was this enough to keep Remco onboard? Yes, it was.

Now that the mist surrounding this has cleared, what exactly was happening? Or was there nothing going on all this time, despite all the murmuring? The main protagonists explain. To start with: during the press conference leading up to the road race at the World Championships, this is what Remco had to say: 'Yes, I'm staying put. As always, there's been a lot of speculation. Some of the information appearing in the media even I didn't know about. Quite amusing to hear and read all of that. But, nothing is changing. I'm staying with my team Soudal-Quick Step, and together with my teammates, I'm going to fight to achieve our goal: winning the Giro and the Tour.'

Patrick Lefevere, as CEO of Soudal-Quick Step, naturally knows how things stood. He explains: 'Of course, there was a grain of truth in all the stories that were doing the rounds. The rumours about Remco's transfer or him being bought out, different teams merging, or even shutting down our own team, these started circulating when Remco first became world champion on the road in Australia. So, back in 2022. Then, a year ago, the rumours intensified. If super-rich people start talking to each other about a new team, a great project could conceivably materialise. It probably wasn't the ideal time for such discussions though. It was all too last minute for those matters to be settled. That's when unrest arose. And people don't like that, people dislike uncertainty, especially in the short term. That's also true for riders; they also need to know how the land lies. There were riders who no longer dared to sign with us, they were afraid to join, they didn't believe that nothing was going on. I've done a lot of people management in recent times. I work with lots of people, and they were in shock when they read and heard that our team might be merging into a larger entity. Those people need to put food on the table, most of them are still young, they have small children, they're paying the mortgage on a new house. I was able to reassure those people.'

Addressing the uncertainty, Patrick Evenepoel says: 'The deal that was supposed to be made with Jumbo-Visma didn't go through. There were a lot of talks, lasting more than a year. Eventually, these turned into talks happening above the heads of the people involved, at a much higher level, with major shareholders and lawyers. In the end, there were indeed proposals on the table, there was talk of Red Bull and INEOS, but ultimately, the most important question was: what's best for Remco? And the answer to that question is: it's what Remco himself wants. That's what's best. Had Remco made certain – other – choices, then it's highly likely that the current team would simply have disappeared. But that was never Remco's intention. Remco wants to achieve his goals, and he would rather do that with the people with whom it all started. Imagine if there'd been a different deal after all, with a transfer or something like that. Imagine if Remco signs with Red Bull, for example. Then all hell would have broken loose. Remco would have received all the blame. Remco is not like that. Remco stays with those with whom he feels comfortable. That's the real Remco.' By the way, Patrick Evenepoel concludes: 'No team had spoken directly with Remco. That would have caused a real mess. No one dared to do that. Talks? They were at a higher level.'

And so, Soudal-Quick Step gained new momentum for the coming years: the team can work on optimising training camps, medical support, and nutrition. Everything needs to be in perfect shape if Remco is to reach his goals.

Patrick Lefevere adds one more thing: 'I was often accused of never being able to build a Tour team. But that's not true. People can only remember for 48 hours, they forget quickly. Enric Mas came second in the Vuelta, Bob Jungels came sixth in the Giro, and Daniel Martin came sixth in the Tour. Each time, we also won a lot of stages. We're looking forward to achieving our thousandth UCI victory in 2025. In 2024, we finished in third place in the UCI team ranking, behind UAE Team Emirates (first) and Visma|Lease A Bike (second). But budget-wise, we weren't in the top six that year. As I say, people are quick to forget, they have short memories. But I can cope with that. I've been through a lot, there's something inside that drives me. What is it? It's difficult for me to explain. I have a thick skin. With a high tolerance for setbacks and a solid sense of perspective, I think I can go a long way.'

29

'THE FIRST TIME,
THERE WERE ABOUT
10 OR 12 OF THEM.
THEY THOUGHT IT WAS
FANTASTIC. A WORLD
WAS OPENING UP
TO THEM.'

It's what fathers and sons do sometimes – you can probably relate to it from what happens in your own home: sitting together on the sofa, in the evening after dinner, there's (still) nothing on TV, chatting about life in general, about the future and what it will bring. Can you picture that scene? You can, right?

It was the same not too long ago with Patrick and Remco – sometime around early 2023. 'What Vincent Kompany has done for football in Brussels, couldn't we do something similar for cycling?' Remco asked from his armchair at home in Schepdaal. Patrick had looked at Remco. He was familiar with Kompany's story.

Vincent Kompany was an outstanding footballer from 2003 to 2020, playing for Anderlecht in Belgium, Hamburger SV in Germany, Manchester City in England, and then Anderlecht again. Kompany was a solid defender, but also a strategist, a leader, a coach on the field – until he became one off the field as well, with Anderlecht at first. After that, he moved to England, where he became coach for Burnley, a somewhat old-fashioned team with a possession-based, attacking style of play, that had just been relegated out of the Premier League and was eager to make an immediate return out of the Championship, the second tier. Kompany succeeded in that endeavour, but things went wrong in the Premier League: Burnley couldn't maintain their position and went down to the lower division. And Kompany? His career took off in a big way and he became the coach of FC Bayern Munich, the powerhouse of the Bundesliga, the best German team there is – all of this happened at the start of the 2024-2025 season. Kompany was (and still is) known for his passion, his desire to bring out the best in his players, and his social engagement – he never denied his roots, growing up as he did in a poorer area of Brussels, the Noordwijk. As a child, Vincent Kompany had personal experience of what it was like to earn his place in a team, at a club, in a group of friends. That served him well from his early days at Anderlecht. He always remembered what he had to do to succeed: trust, encouragement, discipline, and empathy were values that Kompany continued to embrace as pillars on which to base your life. In 2013 – when he was still actively playing football – Vincent made his social engagement explicit: he developed a part-social, part-sporting project that eventually became known as BX Brussels. If you visit the club's website now, you will see his mantra on its homepage: 'Developing Talent On & Off The Pitch'.

'Remco himself also came from football,' says Patrick. 'Back then, he would sometimes see children come to training with torn and tattered sports bag under their arm or football shoes with holes in them. Sometimes those children brought little or nothing to eat or snack on from home. Remco felt that those boys had been left to fend for themselves by their parents. That touched him.'

And so, that evening while sitting on the sofa, Remco decided to set about creating a social cycling project: the R.EV Brussels Cycling Academy was born in his mind and in Patrick's. The Academy has since become a training centre with two key elements. There is the social aspect, which takes place in the Brussels-Capital Region, and there is the sporting aspect, which operates from Schepdaal. The project has a clear structure: on the board of directors are Remco and Patrick, Christoph Impens, Bob Verbeeck, and Anthony Fina from Golazo, the international sports company. It's supported financially by the City of Brussels, the Brussels-Capital Region, and partners such as AG Insurance, 6 Day Sportdrank, Soudal, and Specialized.

Under this management structure of the board of directors, Remco's father coordinates the entire academy – it has now become more of a full-time job. He has a team of regular coaches, nutritionists, mechanics, and volunteers at his disposal.

First, let's take a look at the social aspect...
'This aspect targets community centres and youth clubs in Brussels,' says Patrick. The City of Brussels and the Brussels-Capital Region strong-

ly support this project, they believe in it. It provides young people and children with the opportunity to develop in a playful, yet structured, safe, and nurturing way. 'We presented our plans in the community centres and youth clubs,' says Patrick. Their organisers were pretty enthusiastic. After Patrick and his team's talk, the children could sign up at their community centre for an afternoon of cycling fun. They could try something new which they might enjoy since it was, after all, different from the usual activities they participated in, such as playground activities, theatre, and film. The result was staggering and still is, even more so: the project is booming, with 178 children attending the latest test days in the early autumn of 2024. After school on Wednesdays, with supervision present, the youngsters head for the King Baudouin Stadium in the Belgian capital. There, they learn all about cycling and bikes. They arrive without bikes, as it's not the intention for them to bring their own. It is, after all, an activity within the community programme. On arrival at the stadium, they're given a vest to wear and a bike to use for the afternoon's practice. For many of them, a whole new world opens up, they're not used to such things. 'The first time, there were about 10 or 12 of them,' Remco's father recounts. 'They thought it was fantastic, because the following week there they were again, and some had brought their friends with them, making it some 15 or 18 altogether. Gradually it built up into a wonderful group of 200 or so. It's a diverse group with all kinds of profiles. A cross-section of Brussels youth on bikes, in short.'

Some of the children from the Wednesday club in the Brussels-Capital Region did so well in due course that they were able to join the Academy in Schepdaal. And that brings us neatly to the second aspect of the project: the sporting aspect, which was named the R.EV Cycling Team. On Wednesdays and Sundays, 10 to 14-year-olds – who do not yet hold a licence from the Cycling Federation until they potentially become juniors in the U17 category – are introduced to all aspects of cycling under the guidance of certified coaches. It's not just about how to polish a bike, but also about human values, attitudes, and skills. 'We instil values in those youngsters,' says Patrick. 'And it was Remco who articulated the values the Academy stands for.' What precisely constitutes those values is brought out clearly in their detailed presentation. It concerns personal skills: learning to take responsibility, commitment, trust, (self-)discipline, and intrinsic motivation. But also social skills, like empathy, the ability to communicate well, team spirit, interaction, and so-called methodological skills: the ability to analyse, present oneself, cope with stress, interact with new media, and think critically to solve problems.

It is wonderful and heart-warming to witness what happens in Schepdaal, the location for the sporting aspect: little boys and girls – Patrick's own words – arrive at the meeting spot, a bit uneasy, slightly nervous: perhaps Remco himself might be here; might they get to meet their idol, their role model, in person? And there are plenty of examples of children who arrive in their plimsolls and after just seven months, are clipping into the pedals and showing talent for the sport, for cycling. In Schepdaal, 58 children have now joined the R.EV Cycling Team. The objective? Getting the children competition-ready by the time they can join the U17,' says Patrick. But, he goes on to add: 'Only if they want it for themselves. Because enjoyment, fun, and play remain the most important things.'

But Remco is a winner – as you know. And so, considerable effort is also put into building a team that can pull its weight in competition. In 2025, a junior team needs to be ready to fully participate in Belgium's greatest races, a team that can go on to be an elite team. And honestly speaking, says Patrick: 'It's all looking very promising. We're going to make it happen. Some boys and girls are already participating in national test rides and achieving great results.' What names? Mohammad Ali Kabou, Mathieu Levaque, Rayane Arrifi, Mattéo Van der Schoot, Lobke Spinoy. Also, the Luxembourg youth champion and a strong Norwegian rider are joining the junior team. 'We explained the entire project to the young riders and their parents,' says Patrick. They've been taught about skills such as technique and tactics. They've learned about nutrition and the body itself. The members of the junior team are also immediate role models for their much younger team mates, aged 11 and 12 – 'Look, boys and girls. This is what we've already achieved. And you can do the same, in a few years time.' The juniors come to the initiation sessions for the younger kids and give them a pat on the back. 'That's what makes the Academy so strong,' says Patrick.

By the way, there's something else, says Remco's dad. And he briefly mentions again that Remco decided to stay with his team, Soudal-Quick Step, just before the 2024 World Championship. 'That was also an important signal to those young people. That Remco did this showed respect for the agreements made: remember how you got here, don't break contracts.'

Remco enjoys being with those young riders as he showed by joining them at the Belgian time trial championship and reporting it on social media – in other words, he keeps the project alive. 'We've made more progress in a single year than we ever dreamed possible,' says Patrick. Meanwhile, the sports hall on the Levenslust estate in Schepdaal has been renovated, a bike workshop has been built, new changing rooms are available, and children can now do mountain biking, gymnastics, and athletics there. Target group: again children aged between 10 and 14.

Patrick pours another coffee, with a piece of gingerbread. He is proud of the Academy's accomplishments. For him, it is mainly about how this project is a wonderful amalgamation of education, sporting challenges, focus, friendship, and achievements. And it's true: some parents of the children who come on Wednesdays and Sundays are dreaming of a very bright future – who wouldn't do that for their children (and themselves)? Patrick can always bring perspective to those conversations with parents and children: what do you do with your son or daughter if he or she shows signs of (a lot of) talent? Patrick is honest: 'You end up on a roller coaster where your child is no longer just your child. Overnight, Agna and I went from being just the parents of a child to being the parents of a world champion, an Olympic champion. That's unique because that champion still remains, quite simply, your child, your son.'

It's not easy, Patrick says, to explain all that: how should parents handle a child with so much talent? How should parents respond? What do you do? Patrick can only try and impart his experience of this with the parents of the children at the Academy, both in Brussels and in Schepdaal, no, it's not easy. Yes, it is a roller coaster. 'You have to try and deal with it.' Above all, let the children enjoy themselves, let them discover what they're good at, and perhaps what they aren't good at – that shapes them.

And who knows: maybe one of the children from the Academy will be racing in the World Championship in 2030. A boy or a girl, who started when just 10 years old and then progressed to the U17, to the under-23s, and to the national team squad. Because, indeed that's also the intention of the project: to raise the bar, identify quality, and allow it to develop.

Lobke.
Mattéo.
Arrifi.
Mohammad Ali.
Mathieu.
And the others.
May dream.
Of medals.
Of victories.
Of a great life.

In the run-up to the 2024 World Championship in Zurich, the International Cycling Union (UCI) officially announced that the 2030 Road World Championships would be awarded to Brussels. An imme diate incentive for everyone within the Academy to make their dreams come true: could one of them possibly become a world champion in their very own city?

30

'AMICHE E AMICI BUONGIORNO DA BERGAMO! È IL GIORNO DE IL LOMBARDIA 2024!'

In the north of Italy, Saturday 12 October 2024 was a chilly day. The weather conditions in the preceding week had been apocalyptic. The Tre Valli Varesine – a preparatory race for what was going to be the climax of the year today – was even cancelled on the Tuesday due to the rain, which was so heavy that the water cascaded across the roads, causing them to crack and split. It was eerie, dangerous, impossible. The riders had no inclination to continue riding in those conditions that day. They were right: it had to be abandoned.

But on 12 October, the sky had cleared, and it was sunny in Bergamo. It had turned into a lovely autumn day, after all the previous days' misery. The 118th edition of the Tour of Lombardy was starting in the morning. The riders would cycle all the way to Como, a distance of 255 kilometres, following a fantastic route that winds up and down through mountains and valleys against a background of stunning scenery featuring lakes, ravines, and burbling streams. It's always like that, there in Lombardy.

The official website of the classic went live on Saturday morning. At exactly 9 hours and 19 minutes, it read: *'Amiche e amici buongiorno da Bergamo! È il giorno de Il Lombardia 2024!'*

The Tour of Lombardy was once again extremely difficult, with climbs that have charming names, but are anything but charming: Forcellino di Bianzano, Colle di Berbenno, Sella di Osigo, Madonna del Ghisallo, Colma di Sormano, San Fermo della Battaglia.

It was the last major event of the year 2024. For Remco; it was the final race of the year, big or small. Enough was enough. Remco had indicated that in the previous conversations. He'd said that the batteries were gradually running down. But had immediately added: 'I'm going to give it my all one more time.' The leaves on the trees turn yellow, green, brown, and orange in the autumn, just before they fall – Lombardy is after all known as *'la classica delle foglie morte'*, the race of the dead leaves. Then comes winter, and all is still, calm, and peaceful.

Tadej Pogačar won in Como after 6 hours, 4 minutes, and 58 seconds. It was his fourth victory in a row in the north of Italy. The organisers continued streaming live on their website: *'È la quarta vittoria consecutiva per Tadej come Fausto Coppi!'* The fourth consecutive victory, just as Fausto Coppi had done once, in days gone by, in Lombardy. Three minutes and sixteen seconds later Remco came in second. He raised his hand in the air as he crossed the finish line, rode into Oumi's arms, and they embraced each other warmly. At 16.55 on Saturday evening, 12 October, the phenomenal season of Remco, Oumi, Agna, and Patrick, and the entire team around the young rider, came to a close. Three days later, Remco was awarded the 'Kristallen Fiets' (Crystal Bicycle) – the trophy for the best rider in his country, Belgium. Ten days later, on Tuesday, 22 October, it was announced that Remco had finished the season as second in the UCI World Ranking. Tadej Pogačar was first, and Remco's fellow countryman Jasper Philipsen was third.

A tear fell, and Remco rubbed his eyes with his fingers. He was thinking back to 15 August 2020. On that Saturday, now more than four years ago, it had been warm and sunny in northern Italy. At the time, the world was going through coronavirus, and life was so constrained. There were still just over 40 kilometres to go on that Saturday in August. The riders had ascended the Muro di Sormano, and there was a leading group of seven riders. Then, during the descent, fate struck.

And now, in 2024, Remco had returned to the Muro. He'd already gone back once prior to the race on Saturday, 12 October. Together with Oumi, he'd wanted to see the wall again and in some way or other it had done him good to be there, with his sweetheart. Now he could finally put the fall from that time behind him. Remco and Oumi had silently looked at each other for a moment. How have they been able to be so strong together, with their family, friends, teammates, and sponsors?

It had all turned out well.

It had all turned out better than well.

But now, as evening fell on 12 October 2024, as evening fell, the time for racing was over for a while.

For four weeks, there was no more desire to cycle; it was time to enjoy each other's company and the sheer bliss of doing nothing. It was now time to be together with friends and family: simply being at home, switching roles, and supporting Oumi in *her* final phase of studies, as she worked towards graduating with her master's degree.

That's how it was, right, Remco?

Yes, it was.

31

EPILOGUE

It's nice to be back in the combined shop and coffee bar in Schepdaal again. Patrick is organising an espresso again, and outside the sun is shining it's head off. The weather is beautiful on this very last Friday of October 2024. In the evening, the weatherman will announce in the media that it was the warmest 25th of October since records began: 20.4 degrees in the centre of Belgium. Patrick slices the gingerbread in two and places a piece next to the espresso. After all the conversations in recent months, Patrick knows the author's weaknesses.

'I take a flat white,' says Remco.
'It's my favourite coffee, a double espresso with steamed milk. Nice.'
Remco is in holiday mode – for the past one-and-a-half weeks he hasn't had to do anything, not since the Tour of Lombardy marked the end of a gruelling season. Now Remco can just enjoy himself, tomorrow he's departing for a proper holiday: together with Oumi, he'll spend the next week or two exploring Morocco. But before that, Remco takes a seat for a long chat. And talks frankly.
About life.
About racing.
About family.
And himself.

Yes, Remco says, it's true that he lives *full gas* the entire season, all year long. And he thinks that's normal. He has no other choice. Because, as he says: 'I'm extremely ambitious. My bar is set quite high. And that bar, I set it that high for myself. It's a choice that I make for myself. Am I striving for perfection? Yes, that too is true. If I want to win races, I can't just do that with my eyes closed. Winning has to be worked on, there needs to be structure in which to do that, and a framework in which I can operate. That's how it is. I don't do just any old thing.' Remco takes a sip of his coffee and says: 'That pursuit of perfection, that's definitely characteristic of me, I believe.'

That there's a good head on this guy's shoulders, is what the people featured in this book have said – 'Remco races with his legs, but also with his head. How he does that, it's unimaginable, you know. Strong or not, confident or not, the legs often do what the mind tells them.' Remco knows that they say that about him. But how exactly did that strong mind come to be? 'I've no idea, actually,' he says. 'Maybe it has to do with the fact that I've been competing in sports at a high level from a very young age. I've been committed, focused, and wanting to perform from the very beginning.' And there's something else, Remco says: 'I'm an only child, and both my parents were hard-working, self-employed persons who didn't watch the clock; they were always busy doing something. I learnt to fend for myself. My iron will must have been developing even then.' Remco chose to become a cyclist and left football behind. He became an instant success on the bike; Remco was immediately a great cyclist. 'In your youth, the idea that you're a great rider can quite easily start to play in your mind. All too soon you start thinking like that, especially when you win this and that. But after the European Championship in the summer of 2018, it did really look like I had a future as a professional cyclist. And that was definitely the case after the World Championship. Those were the moments when I knew: OK, I'm going to become a pro, and perhaps even a good one. What I *didn't* know back then was where the final destination would be. Although I was quickly among the two or three best riders in the world, I still had to discover for myself the steps I needed to take to get to the top. I'm not the kind of person who thinks everything will fall into place on its own. I also want to perfectly mark out the route to a goal for myself. I take conscious steps.' Remco sees the way in which he managed the days following the Paris Olympics as the best example of this. 'After winning my two gold medals, I immediately set my sights on performing well at the World Championships too. I'd taken a couple of days off after the Games, but still: I wanted to complete my goals for the year. I wanted to perform at the World Championship, and I also want to do the same in Lombardy. As long as the season is still going on, I continue to set goals for myself. That's how it's going to be throughout my career: I will always be up for a new challenge. Striving for my goals and pursuing perfection are equally as important as reaching the final destination. That's simply how I'm made.'

The fact that Remco secured another gold medal in the road race just a week after his first in the time trial showed he wasn't affected by a lost motivation – that psychological phenomenon whereby, following a peak performance, the mind tells you it's OK to ease off and release the pressure. Remco can confirm that: 'I'm very good at going from one extreme effort to another one, and doing it in a trice. The day after the Olympic Games, I was already lounging by a pool, with nothing to do – just for a few days, less than a week. That's also the case now, at the end of October: the entire season has been *full gas* all the way, in terms of nutrition and training and travel. I push myself to the limits in terms of sport. Now, during the break, I'm pushing myself to the limits as a human being. I can now do everything that's not good for my sport. I don't have to be an athlete for a while; I'm just an ordinary person now.'

Be careful, Remco says: Don't get thinking I'll throw myself into parties; I'm not getting into alcohol. 'I can now spend the whole day lounging on the sofa, or enjoying a breakfast together with Oumi, with nothing but pastries in the morning. Yeah, *temporarily*, living freely, with minimal restrictions. Taking it easy *temporarily*, letting my mind be empty, free of plans, for a few days, no *full gas* for a bit, ignoring messages and not answering the phone. My parents will be able to confirm that. Taking full advantage of it, *temporarily*. Then I'll stop doing that and it will be time to refocus.'

Such a moment of '*temporarily* not' also occurred after the time trial at the Paris Games. There had been a short celebration, together with Wout van Aert, a brief appearance on the podium at the Belgian House, a moment to please the team's entourage. 'And then I went home by car. I got to bed at 3 o'clock in the morning. I stayed home for two days, did absolutely nothing, just some easy riding. I completely relaxed. I was ready for a new focus.

On 3 August 2024, Remco became Olympic champion again. He chuckles gently. Remembering that achievement, no doubt. Recalling that glorious moment when he stepped off the bike, raised his hands in the air, and spread his arms. But Remco also chuckles gently at the fond memory of what followed, after his victorious ride on the course through the city, past Montmartre, the Eiffel Tower, and all those other wonderful places. He thinks back to the moment when, hours after the finish, he walked through the streets of Paris, on his way to the hotel, not far from the airport. There, walking through the City of Light with Oumi and her brothers, who had accompanied her to the race, Remco was looking for something to eat, something he hadn't had the opportunity to do yet – it was already quite late in the evening. Or more precisely in the nighttime, and Remco was feeling rather hungry, not surprisingly after his exertion. Suddenly, they came across a place that was still open, and food was still available. Five minutes later they were all tucking into a kebab. When they looked up, they could see the Arc de Triomphe. 'There we sat at 3 o'clock in the morning, right in the heart of Paris, with no one bothering us, without being disturbed. That was a unique moment,' says Remco. 'That did me so much good, the peace and quiet, and the kebab. I was able to take a moment and let what I had achieved sink in, to fully comprehend it myself. That meant more to me than any official duty whatsoever, where I have to go from the umpteenth photo session to yet another interview without having the chance to savour what just happened.' The next day, Monday, 4 August, Remco went for a meal at a decent brasserie. 'With my parents, my grandparents and Oumi. Ordinary, comfortable. Nothing special.' What does that say about him, that he takes such pleasure in the little things, the small moments of happiness? 'That I will never live beyond my means,' Remco says with conviction. 'I know I make a good living, but I'm not going to spend it on cars, expensive watches, or who knows what. That's not me.'

Meanwhile, Remco allowed people to dream, he did what Fred Vandervennet had told him to do: 'Let people dream, Remco. Give them something to be happy about.' Remco ponders for a moment and then says: 'Yes, after the Games, I noticed that I had brought out a lot of emotions in people. That's great, but it doesn't put any extra pressure on me. It's outside my control, anyway.' Remco pauses to think and then goes on to say: 'Since getting married to Oumi, I have a different mindset. It has to do with the Arabic culture she has introduced me to. Thanks to Oumi, I've learned that I should only control what is controllable. That was difficult in the beginning because I was a different person before my marriage. After my fall in Lombardy, for example, I wanted too much, too quickly. I was impatient. When I realised that I could look at things more calmly, I started performing better and broke through to the highest possible level. I'll give an example: this year, I wasn't in good form in the Tour of England, or rather, I was performing badly by my standards. A few years ago, I would have come out of that race feeling stressed. I've come to understand now that those bad days were part of a process I had to go through to become better. I could turn things around. The result? I became world champion in the time trial in Zurich, finished fifth in the road race, and second in Lombardy.' So, has he become more mature then? 'It was a gradual change after 2021. Up until then, I would alternate between a good day and a bad week, and a good month with yet another bad day.' And there had been the terrible fall in Lombardy. 'I wanted to come back too quickly then, but in the end it showed that I wasn't done with racing yet. No matter how severe the fall and its consequences had been, I didn't want to give up.' Remco reflects: 'It took a long time for me to feel comfortable again.' He pauses momentarily and then says: 'Lombardy was a good lesson. It taught me that I had an incredible amount of resilience. But above all: I was still here, I was still alive. I was with the people I loved, with my family, those with whom I can be myself and release all my feelings, those with whom I don't have to hold back. I could still cherish them and enjoy the little things.' Holding his coffee, Remco says: 'Little things, it doesn't have to be about big things all the time. People are inclined to forget that.'

In 2022, Remco won Liège-Bastogne-Liège and the Vuelta, and became world champion in the road race in Australia. 'Everything went perfectly, I'd shown what I was capable of, the pressure had disappeared: now I could truly *deliver* what was expected of me. At that moment, a completely different Remco came into being. More mature? Maybe so.' Remco looks ahead, takes a sip of his coffee, and says: 'Yes, I have changed over the years. It's been a process that I've gone through. At the start of my career, I wasn't afraid to put myself under a lot of pressure, be the tough guy. And I know that people sometimes found it hard to understand me, I dared to assert myself, even in the media. I heard that people perceived me to be arrogant. I realise now that perhaps I brought those reactions on myself. But people have since realised that I also do what I say. And my ego no longer has the upper hand. I can now admit, for example, that I wasn't good enough to beat Tadej.' Remco repeats once again: 'Yes, I have changed over the years. And many of those who were against me in the beginning have since turned into supporters.' Remco wants to illustrate that changed behaviour a bit more clearly. He takes you, dear reader, to the start podium at the 2024 World Time Trial Championship in the summer. 'Those images of my chain falling off show perfectly who I am at the moment,' he says. 'When that malfunction happened, I was fuming, inside and outside. I tried to suppress the inner fumes immediately, I did that with my tough mindset, with my mental strength. There was no point in getting worked up inside. I stayed calm, and that fed through to the people who wanted to help me. I did react briefly to the cameraman because he'd come much too close. He was after creating drama, and that wasn't right. So, I wasn't going to ignore it. That minute showed perfectly who I've become: I was ready to perform but something had happened that couldn't be controlled, I accepted it, and all I could do was hope for the best.' Remco channelled the external fumes for an hour, riding purely on instinct, with no power meter, relying solely on the time differences he managed to hear along the route. He became world champion.

Let's go back to Remco's motto for a moment: in pursuit of perfection... 'I know the course of a race, I know what to expect,' says Remco. 'I know the reference points I can use for guidance. I know the difficult sections where I need to pay extra attention. On the day when it needs to happen, I want to be as well-prepared as possible. Is that the pursuit of perfection? Yes. In my mind, I know exactly the sections where I want to push it, where I can go all out, and where I can recover for a moment. The preparation for a race day is like the preparation for an exam. It *has* to happen on that day. In the race, I'm focused exclusively on the race, I don't think about other things. The focus on the competition is the only thing that counts. For example, I know that after one kilometre, there will be a downhill section that involves a one-minute descent where I can take some pressure off my legs. I knew for instance that there'd be a section on the flat at the Olympics. I knew that the 1'20" before that was really tough. If I dropped the Frenchman who was still with me and kept pushing hard, I knew he probably wouldn't be able to catch me up again. And I judged that accurately. Or again: also at the Olympics – the race had been tough for 10, 15 minutes. For classic riders, such a time-span is often their limit. That's how long they can keep going *full gas*. I'm more of an all-rounder and time trial rider. When the classic riders reach their limit, I can still keep going.'

Remco laughs: 'Just like Tadej. He too has that capability.'
'A fantastic cyclist, in a fantastic generation. That makes for fun. But sometimes it's also a bit frustrating. I know I'm often better than the rest, I'm riding at an exceptional level. But then again, there's another who's even better. Pogačar. So then I ask myself: how can I get to his level? That's annoying: indeed, how can I aspire to that level? But at the same time, it has its positive side: I can turn that challenge into a goal.' In any case, the top riders respect each other's victories, says Remco. 'Because we know what it takes to achieve them and the sacrifices involved. You don't win without putting in the work. And there are a lot of other influential factors: the pressure, your health, luck. We all know that. And then you have to accept the victories of the others.'

Remco is 24 years old, in 2024. 'I realise that in the course of three, four years, it has progressed rapidly, from nothing to everything. I've already had an incredible career. Yes, I realise that. But I haven't yet achieved all my goals in cycling. In the beginning, it was my intention to win the three Grand Tours someday – that was my initial goal. In the meantime, I've already won the Tour of Spain, which is great. But when all is said and done, it won't be enough to satisfy me. My initial goal is also my ultimate goal: victory in the Tour, the Giro, and the Vuelta. Only then will the circle be complete for me. I know that I've made my circle a really big one, I'm very conscious of that. But I've done that because I know it's within my capability. If, at the end of my journey, I've only won three of the Grand Tours, then I'm going to be disappointed with myself. Because then my circle will be incomplete.'

What will Remco be doing when he is, let's say, 34 or 44? 'Gosh,' he says, 'a good question.' The flat white is almost finished, just one final sip, just a little longer, to the end of this book. 'I'm not thinking about that now, about what will happen to me in some 10 or 20 years. I can't worry about that right now. I have too much on my mind right now, I'm fully focused on racing. If I were to think about that presently, then it would be a distraction. It would start to get inside my head. That's not good. Right now, I'm doing everything for my cycling career, no half measures. I want to invest as much as I can in that, I want to create a stable foundation.'

The author has finished off his espresso and gingerbread.
Father Patrick has been listening in.
Remco has a meeting shortly.
The journey awaits tomorrow, and then the holiday will start in earnest.

'Nope,' he says.
'A foundation that lacks stability, that doesn't work.'
'I won't build anything on shifting sands.'
'*Full gas*, is how I do things.'
'I'm striving for perfection.'

Schepdaal, 25 October 2024

ACKNOWLEDGEMENTS

I worked on this book, this story, during the spring and summer of 2024.

I immersed myself in all things Remco at the end of March: his life, his victories, his injuries, his triumphs, his actions and behaviour. It became a journey that continued well into the autumn. Who could have thought there would be so many remarkable achievements to cover? Who would have thought that so many people would open up their hearts to me? I am indebted to Patrick and Agna, Remco's parents, for the fact that so many people wanted to tell their story. They believed in me and in my book from the very start. Patrick and I spent many an hour together, with Agna supporting from behind the scenes and serving as the moral compass of this story. You have my heartfelt gratitude!

I drank a lot of coffee, with Kevin and another Patrick, with Carlo and Fred, with Jef and one more Patrick, with Yannick and yet another Patrick, with Toon. I talked to people in distant countries, such as Mike and Matxin. I want to thank each and every one of them, I hope we can enjoy a coffee together somewhere, sometime in the future.

All these months, I've had my mind on Remco, thinking what he thought, following him in the Tour, at the Olympics, in the Basque Country and Lombardy, in Schepdaal, and all those other places. Even at home, I was absent so to speak. My family knows my thoughts were elsewhere then. They know that although they can see me at my desk, I'm actually in the Pyrenees, or in the Alps, or in the final kilometre of a time trial, as it were. I want to thank Carla, Bram, Louise, and Dries for their understanding (and support). From next week onwards, it'll be me who puts out the rubbish sacks again, I promise (more or less).

The people at Lannoo believed in this book and the way in which I wanted to approach this project. Johan, Yaele, Hilde, and Mathilde kept me company through my experiences and those of Remco. I'm really grateful that you did.

And I want to express my thanks to two wonderful people in particular: Remco and Oumi. They let me enter their world, their lives. I've learned things from them, it was a pleasure getting to know them.

I hope you enjoy this book, dear reader.

www.lannoo.com

Register on our website and we will regularly send you a newsletter with information about new books and interesting, exclusive offers.

Text	Filip Osselaer
Images	belga
Translation	James Duncan
Design	Koen Surmont, windwaait.be
Typesetting	banananas.net

If you have observations or questions, please contact our editorial office:
redactielifestyle@lannoo.com

© Filip Osselaer – Uitgeverij Lannoo nv, Tielt, 2024
D/2024/45/582 – NUR 480/491
ISBN 978-90-209-5056-4